The Greenleaf Guide to Ancient Literature

An Inductive Approach

By Cyndy Shearer

Greenleaf Press
Lebanon, Tennessee

With thanks to my beloved guinea pigs, both birthed and borrowed,
who diligently studied this course with me over the last six years.
What would we have done without the "Ice Queen?"
And to Janine MacIvor whose proofing help was a Godsend.
Any remaining errors slipped in while we slept, will be corrected in the next edition,
and are not Janine's fault.

Internet: www.greenleafpress.com
3761 Highway 109N, Unit D
Lebanon, Tennessee 37087
615-449-1617

GReenLeaf
P·R·E·S·S

Visit our website for further information:
http://www.greenleafpress.com

Contents

A Note to the teacher

If you are teaching more than one grade level, maybe several grade levels; and *if*, in addition to that, you have young children demanding your full attention; ***and if*** you were *not* a college literature major, never *went* to college, or have very little desire to *read,* much less *teach* Ancient Literature, you might be tempted to just hand your high school student the books and study guide for this course and tell them to answer the questions in writing and turn it all in when he or she is done. You may have signed your teen up for a co-op or tutorial class in which your student will meet together once a week to discuss this material with other students and a teacher who really (somehow) enjoys this stuff. You may feel you don't have the time, the interest, or the ability to read the material. If you have said, "Yes," "Amen," or "Preach it, sister," to any or all of the above, then this introduction is especially for you!

One of the greatest joys of homeschooling my own children has been the opportunity to spend time studying **with** them. There have been many, many times when I have not come to a subject with a whole lot of prior knowledge or enthusiasm, and we have been learning together as we go. The time spent discussing, experimenting, and working through projects together has been invaluable time. Not only did we learn new things, but we built a relationship and made some pretty special memories. As our family has gotten bigger, and as the age span has broadened (20-2, as of right now), it has been harder and harder to do this. When your family includes high schoolers and little ones, it seems almost impossible to find the time. However, the rewards for taking the time to continue to learn along with your high school student are great.

Here are just some of the issues you will have a chance to talk about as you study Ancient Literature in this course:

- Man's beginnings according to Genesis and Romans 1.
- The differences between the Biblical account of early man and the evolutionary view.
- A Biblically based apologetic (or defense) for the study of cultures (ancient ones like Babylon and Greece, in particular) by way of Daniel's example.
- How God's character differs from the character of the gods of the Babylonians/Sumerians/Assyrians and Greeks.
- Heroism. What is a true hero? What makes a person great?
- Man's relationship to God Biblically and in the pagan world.

2

- The differences between wisdom and cunning.
- The Question of Fate – what determines a man's fate and what can one do to alter that fate? How much responsibility does a person have for the way life turns out?
- What is the Biblical relationship between the individual and the state and God? What about civil disobedience?

None of these are light-weight issues! The way in which a person responds to each of these issues tells quite a bit about that person's view of the world. As your teen thinks about these things he or she is forming his or her own world view. Most of us homeschool because we want to be involved in the shaping of our children's character and their view of the world. However your student is using this material, I encourage you to use this course as a tool toward that end.

If your teen had a chance to tour Europe without you, you could still share in the trip through postcards, photographs, videos and letters. But nothing could ever even come close to the experience of traveling along together. In the same way, you might assign readings and have your teens write summaries of reading material, answer discussion questions, or simply tell you what they've read. These activities would demonstrate their mastery of the material. But, if you are reading along with them, the quality of your time together will be so much richer! Although it is possible for your student to do this course fairly independently, let me encourage you to study together. In fact, I would encourage you to either buy your own copy of this guide (or make one copy of it, if you have access to a cheap enough copier) for yourself, and do the assigned readings and work along with your student– fill out the pages, even.

The postcards would show you what your traveling teen had seen, and the shortcuts will still get your teen to graduation, but how much better to make the trip together!

Why an *inductive* study of literature?

In any discipline, there are two methods of study—deductive and inductive.

Deductive Method:

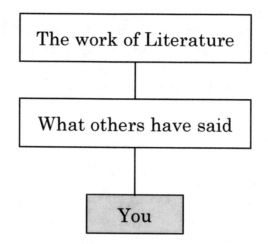

In a deductive approach to literature, you generally will begin your study of a work by reading what others have said about it. You might read some introductory background information, a summary of the main action of the piece, someone's analysis of the theme, the plot, the characters. Once you have read *about* what the piece means, you, yourself, read the piece.

Inductive Method:

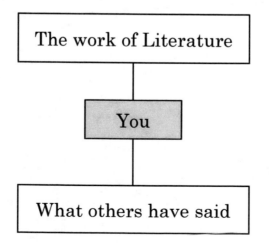

In an inductive approach to literature, you basically reverse the process. While you may start by reading some background information—filling you in on what the original audience would have known as they read or watched the piece performed—the focus of your study begins not with finding out how *others* have interpreted the work, but with reading the work for *yourself.*

There are three steps to any inductive study: **observation, interpretation, and application.**

```
┌─────────────────────────────────────────────────────┐
│       3. APPLICATION (SO WHAT DOES IT MATTER?)        │
└─────────────────────────────────────────────────────┘
┌─────────────────────────────────────────────────────┐
│    2. INTERPRETATION    (WHAT DOES IT MEAN?)          │
└─────────────────────────────────────────────────────┘
┌─────────────────────────────────────────────────────┐
│  1. OBSERVATION   (WHAT DOES IT SAY?)                 │
└─────────────────────────────────────────────────────┘
```

The observation step is the foundation of your study. Without correct observation, your interpretation will be faulty, and any conclusions you might draw will be incorrect.

As you observe the text, you will begin to notice repetitions of words and phrases, sometimes sounds, images, actions, or events. Because a writer will use repetition as a way to emphasize the significance of a thing, you will want to take note of any repetitions you notice. Repetition will lead you to the theme of a piece. Also pay attention to things that are compared and things that are contrasted.

Interpretation must be built on careful observation. You will take all you have observed and begin to analyze. What is the significance of those repeated words or actions? Why are those things compared or contrasted? Why does the writer choose those particular contrasts or comparisons? What point is he or she trying to make? What does the piece mean? What questions is the writer asking? Does the writer provide you with answers for the questions? Does the writer seem to believe there *are* answers for the questions?

In making applications you draw conclusions about what you have just read. So what does the work matter, anyway? How does this material relate to life? How does the writer's point of view (world view) compare with a Scriptural world view? How do the conclusions the writer offers compare with Scripture? How does this material relate to literature as a whole? Does the writer succeed in what he or she was trying to accomplish with this piece? Is this work any good? Is it merely good, or is it great?

After you have read the work yourself, and have begun to formulate your own conclusions, it is helpful to read what others who have studied the same text have said about it. By waiting until the end of your study to read others' opinions, you will be able to evaluate *their* opinions. Do you agree or disagree with their conclusion? How do their conclusions compare to your own conclusions? Have they seen things that you missed? Have you seen things they have missed? Take what you have observed, what others have written, and then by evaluating your own first impressions, draw your own final conclusions.

This is the kind of literary study that will prepare you to speak to the questions your culture is asking. Don't settle for a surface reading "for the test." (You will be bored stiff!) As Daniel and his friends studied the language and literature of the Chaldeans, they studied diligently. As they studied, "God gave them knowledge and skill in all learning and wisdom." (Daniel 1:17) And when they stood before the king, Daniel 1:19-20 says,

> among them all was found none like Daniel, Hananiah, Mishael and Azariah: therefore they stood before the king. And in all matters of wisdom [and] understanding that the king inquired of them, he found them ten times better than all the magicians [and] astrologers that [were] in all his realm.

Make Daniel and his three friends your models as you study. Ask God to give you "knowledge and skill in all learning and wisdom" so that you will be prepared to stand before your culture and *credibly* speak God's message.

Suggested Schedule:

This study is made up of 24 lessons.
Daniel, Genesis, and *The Epic of Gilgamesh* 4 lessons
The Odyssey 4 lessons
Oedipus 5 lessons
Antigone 5 lessons
Anouilh's *Antigone* 5 lessons
Final Summary Assignment 1 lesson

Each of these lessons should take about a week of daily study to complete. For the final summary assignment I would allot two weeks.

For a 36-week school year:

You could simply allow more time for your student to complete a lesson (about a week and a half).
OR
You could assign some written essay or research assignment between each section. Allot approximately 2 weeks per written assignment. There is a lot to be said for taking the time to reflect on what you have just read. Too often students finish one work only to jump immediately into another. They are not given any time to absorb the material, to reflect on it with any depth. I would encourage you to avoid a schedule that rushes your student from one work of literature to the next—the great cattle drive approach. Assigning some sort of reaction paper– whether it is a short essay or a formal research project would be a valuable use of time.

For a 30-week school year:
Allot one week between sections.

Lesson One
Daniel, Chapters 1-4

Texts you will read in this course:

> *The Epic of Gilgamesh*
> *The Odyssey,* Homer
> *Oedipus,* Sophocles
> *Oedipus at Colonus* (selections), Sophocles
> *Antigone,* Sophocles
> *Antigone,* Jean Anouilh

As you can see after looking over the list of texts you will be studying in this course, we'll spend most of our time studying pagan literature. *The Epic of Gilgamesh* is a Babylonian flood story that has much in common with the account of Noah's flood given in Genesis. *The Odyssey* is the second epic poem the Greek poet, Homer, wrote about the Trojan War. The first part, *The Iliad* tells the story of the war itself. As it ends, all of the Greek forces leave for their homes. *The Odyssey* tells the story of one Greek general, Ulysses, or Odysseus, as he struggles to return to his home and family.

Since the writers of these works were neither Jewish nor Christian, they are obviously unconcerned about violating Old Testament prohibitions against idol worship. The stories told by the Babylonian writer of *Gilgamesh* and the Greek poet, Homer, were consistent with the Babylonian and Greek understandings about who the gods were. So how can studying these things be of any benefit to a Christian? Can a Christian even read the stuff in "good faith," so to speak?

This is a serious question. It is important for you to have a clear and Biblically accurate answer to it, before you begin your study.

1. Read Deuteronomy 18:9-12.

2. List the activities or people God says we are to avoid.
   After you make this list, I would recommend that you highlight it in your own Bible and memorize at least the reference, if not the whole passage. Chances are you will need to refer to it again, yourself. You will probably have more than one occasion to take others there as well.

3. What can you learn from Deuteronomy about how we should **not** approach ancient literature, writings, or culture?

4. Can you think of any examples of Godly men who knew something about pagan culture?

5. Read Acts 7:22. Who is described in this verse? How is he described?

Background Information:

An educated Greek was expected to know the Greek Poets, and to quote them in conversation. By demonstrating his familiarity with the poets, he would show that he was a educated, cultured, and thus gave him credibility with his peers.

---

6. Read Acts 17:16-34. Who do you read about in this passage? What is he doing? How would you describe his knowledge and understanding of Greek religion and culture? What use does he make of this knowledge?

7. The next section of this worksheet will ask you to read through Daniel chapters 1-4. It is reprinted here so that as you read, you can mark certain things in the text.

   The next few questions will ask you to read a section of Daniel more than once. (Some of you will think, "AHA! I can read it through once and just look for all the answers the first time!" And you might be able to do that, BUT there are some advantages to doing it the hard way. Each time you read through the text, you will become more and more familiar with the passage. And each time you read through it, you will see things you hadn't noticed before. You will shortchange yourself if you only skim the surface for the most obvious answers.

8. Read through each of the four chapters of Daniel. Find out WHEN the story takes place. Underline those words or phrases that tell you WHEN, and record your findings on the appropriate "Daniel Overview" charts beginning on page 17.

9. Read through each of the four chapters and find out WHERE the story takes place. Draw a box around all the places the writer mentions. Now list those places in the appropriate "Daniel Overview" chart.

10. Read through each of the four chapters and circle the names of all the PEOPLE mentioned in the text. Anytime you see a reference to God, draw a triangle around His Name (or pronouns that refer to Him). List these in the appropriate "Daniel Overview" chart.

11. **Now read Chapter 1 again carefully**.

12. What does Nebuchadnezzar decree?

13. What does that decree mean for Daniel and his friends?

14. How does Daniel respond to the news of the decree?

15. What does Daniel refuse to do? Why does he refuse?

16. What does he *not* refuse to do?

17. Notice Daniel's attitude throughout this chapter. How would you describe it?

18. **Read Chapter 1 again once more.**
    Mark every time God does something. What do you learn about God from this? (Remember these observations. We will come back to them later as we study *The Epic of Gilgamesh* and compare God's character with the character of the gods worshipped by the Babylonians.

19. What kind of contact does Nebuchadnezzar have with the four Hebrews? How does he respond to them?

20. Read Daniel 2:9. Review the entries you made in the Overview Chart for Chapter 2. Notice when and where the events of this chapter take place. Notice who is involved.

21. As Chapter 2 opens, what has just happened? Who is called before the king?

22. What do we learn about Nebuchadnezzar? His wise men? His relationship with his wise men?

23. What does Nebuchadnezzar ask of his wise men this time?

24. How do they respond to his demand? What do they ask him to give them?

25. How does Nebuchadnezzar respond to their request?

26. Read verses 14-16 of chapter 2. Compare Nebuchadnezzar's response to the wise men's request for more time with his response to Daniel's request for more time.

27. Why do you think he responds differently to Daniel?
    (Hint: check Chapter 1 again.)

28. Read verses 17-49 of chapter 2. Especially notice the king's response to Daniel's interpretation in verses 46-49.

29. How do you think this story would have been different if Daniel and his friends had been lazy students?

30. Read Daniel 3 and 4. Notice Nebuchadnezzar's response to the God of Heaven. Who is the author of Daniel Chapter 4?

Application Time!

If you, as a student, were to adopt Daniel as your model, what would that mean for you? How would that affect the way you approach your course work? Your purpose for study? The quality of your work?

How was God able to use Daniel *because* he excelled?

Think about the way the educated pagan world often sees Christians.

If Christians followed Daniel's example, how might that opinion change?

A Challenge and Exhortation to everyone doing this study:

If you read further, you will find that not everyone loves Daniel like Nebuchadnezzar does. In Daniel 6, Daniel runs into a group of folks who resent him because he is respected by those in authority. Because they are jealous of his success, they want him dead. There are lessons to be learned from both Nebuchadnezzar's and the jealous official's reactions to Daniel. But that's another study...

I believe God was able to use Daniel in Nebuchadnezzar's life because of two things. Daniel had an unshakable commitment to obeying God. He knew the Scriptures and was determined to remain faithful to their teachings. He feared God more than he feared any man. Secondly, Daniel was faithful in his Babylonian studies—language, literature, and customs of that culture. Daniel excelled in his studies. He was able to speak clearly to Nebuchadnezzar about the God of Heaven in terms that Nebuchadnezzar understood. When Nebuchadnezzar looked at Daniel, he saw a young man of integrity and diligence. He knew that Daniel could be trusted. Similarly, Paul was able to stand at Mars Hill and speak clearly to the Greeks about the One True God in terms that they understood. How are you preparing yourself to speak to your culture about the Gospel?

DANIEL OVERVIEW CHART – CHAPTER 1

WHEN?

WHERE?   WHAT HAPPENS HERE?

WHO IS MENTIONED?   WHAT IS SAID ABOUT THEM?

DANIEL OVERVIEW CHART – CHAPTER 2

WHEN?

WHERE?   WHAT HAPPENS HERE?

WHO IS MENTIONED?   WHAT IS SAID ABOUT THEM?

DANIEL OVERVIEW CHART – CHAPTER 3

WHEN?

WHERE?

WHAT HAPPENS HERE?

WHO IS MENTIONED?

WHAT IS SAID ABOUT THEM?

DANIEL OVERVIEW CHART -- CHAPTER 4

WHEN?

WHERE?   WHAT HAPPENS HERE?

WHO IS MENTIONED?   WHAT IS SAID ABOUT THEM?

Daniel 1

1 In the third year of the reign of Jehoiakim king of Judah, Nebuchadnezzar king of Babylon came to Jerusalem and besieged it.

2 And the Lord gave Jehoiakim king of Judah into his hand, along with some of the vessels of the house of God; and he brought them to the land of Shinar, to the house of his god, and he brought the vessels into the treasury of his god.

3 Then the king ordered Ashpenaz, the chief of his officials, to bring in some of the sons of Israel, including some of the royal family and of the nobles,

4 youths in whom was no defect, who were good-looking, showing intelligence in every [branch of] wisdom, endowed with understanding, and discerning knowledge, and who had ability for serving in the king's court; and [he ordered him] to teach them the literature and language of the Chaldeans.

5 And the king appointed for them a daily ration from the king's choice food and from the wine which he drank, and [appointed] that they should be educated three years, at the end of which they were to enter the king's personal service.

6 Now among them from the sons of Judah were Daniel, Hananiah, Mishael and Azariah.

7 Then the commander of the officials assigned [new] names to them; and to Daniel he assigned [the name] Belteshazzar, to Hananiah Shadrach, to Mishael Meshach, and to Azariah Abed-nego.

8 But Daniel made up his mind that he would not defile himself with the king's choice food or with the wine which he drank; so he sought [permission] from the commander of the officials that he might not defile himself.

9 Now God granted Daniel favor and compassion in the sight of the commander of the officials,

10 and the commander of the officials said to Daniel, "I am afraid of my lord the king, who has appointed your food and your drink; for why should he see your faces looking more haggard than the youths who are your own age? Then you would make me forfeit my head to the king."

11 But Daniel said to the overseer whom the commander of the officials had appointed over Daniel, Hananiah, Mishael and Azariah,

12 "Please test your servants for ten days, and let us be given some vegetables to eat and water to drink.

13 "Then let our appearance be observed in your presence, and the appearance of the youths who are eating the king's choice food; and deal with your servants according to what you see."

14 So he listened to them in this matter and tested them for ten days.

15 And at the end of ten days their appearance seemed better and they were fatter than all the youths who had been eating the king's choice food.

16 So the overseer continued to withhold their choice food and the wine they were to drink, and kept giving them vegetables.

17 And as for these four youths, God gave them knowledge and intelligence in every [branch of] literature and wisdom; Daniel even understood all [kinds of] visions and dreams.

18 Then at the end of the days which the king had specified for presenting them, the commander of the officials presented them before Nebuchadnezzar.

19 And the king talked with them, and out of them all not one was found like Daniel, Hananiah, Mishael and Azariah; so they entered the king's personal service.

20 And as for every matter of wisdom and understanding about which the king consulted them, he found them ten times better than all the magicians [and] conjurers who [were] in all his realm.

21 And Daniel continued until the first year of Cyrus the king.

Daniel 2

1 Now in the second year of the reign of Nebuchadnezzar, Nebuchadnezzar had dreams; and his spirit was troubled and his sleep left him.

2 Then the king gave orders to call in the magicians, the conjurers, the sorcerers and the Chaldeans, to tell the king his dreams. So they came in and stood before the king.

3 And the king said to them, "I had a dream, and my spirit is anxious to understand the dream."

4 Then the Chaldeans spoke to the king in Aramaic: "O king, live forever! Tell the dream to your servants, and we will declare the interpretation."

5 The king answered and said to the Chaldeans, "The command from me is firm: if you do not make known to me the dream and its interpretation, you will be torn limb from limb, and your houses will be made a rubbish heap.

6 "But if you declare the dream and its interpretation, you will receive from me gifts and a reward and great honor; therefore declare to me the dream and its interpretation."

7 They answered a second time and said, "Let the king tell the dream to his servants, and we will declare the interpretation."

8 The king answered and said, "I know for certain that you are bargaining for time, inasmuch as you have seen that the command from me is firm,

9 that if you do not make the dream known to me, there is only one decree for you. For you have agreed together to speak lying and corrupt words before me until the situation is changed; therefore tell me the dream, that I may know that you can declare to me its interpretation. "

10 The Chaldeans answered the king and said, "There is not a man on earth who could declare the matter for the king, inasmuch as no great king or ruler has [ever] asked anything like this of any magician, conjurer or Chaldean.

11 "Moreover, the thing which the king demands is difficult, and there is no one else who could declare it to the king except gods, whose dwelling place is not with [mortal] flesh."

12 Because of this the king became indignant and very furious, and gave orders to destroy all the wise men of Babylon.

13 So the decree went forth that the wise men should be slain; and they looked for Daniel and his friends to kill [them.]

14 Then Daniel replied with discretion and discernment to Arioch, the captain of the king's bodyguard, who had gone forth to slay the wise men of Babylon;

15 he answered and said to Arioch, the king's commander, "For what reason is the decree from the king [so] urgent?" Then Arioch informed Daniel about the matter.

16 So Daniel went in and requested of the king that he would give him time, in order that he might declare the interpretation to the king.

17 Then Daniel went to his house and informed his friends, Hananiah, Mishael and Azariah, about the matter,

18 in order that they might request compassion from the God of heaven concerning this mystery, so that Daniel and his friends might not be destroyed with the rest of the wise men of Babylon.

19 Then the mystery was revealed to Daniel in a night vision. Then Daniel blessed the God of heaven;

20 Daniel answered and said, "Let the name of God be blessed forever and ever, For wisdom and power belong to Him.

21 "And it is He who changes the times and the epochs; He removes kings and establishes kings; He gives wisdom to wise men, And knowledge to men of understanding.

22 "It is He who reveals the profound and hidden things; He knows what is in the darkness, And the light dwells with Him.

23 "To Thee, O God of my fathers, I give thanks and praise, For Thou hast given me wisdom and power; Even now Thou hast made known to me what we requested of Thee, For Thou hast made known to us the king's matter."

24 Therefore, Daniel went in to Arioch, whom the king had appointed to destroy the wise men of Babylon; he went and spoke to him as follows: "Do not destroy the wise men of Babylon! Take me into the king's presence, and I will declare the interpretation to the king."

25 Then Arioch hurriedly brought Daniel into the king's presence and spoke to him as follows: "I have found a man among the exiles from Judah who can make the interpretation known to the king!"

26 The king answered and said to Daniel, whose name was Belteshazzar, "Are you able to make known to me the dream which I have seen and its interpretation?"

27 Daniel answered before the king and said, "As for the mystery about which the king has inquired, neither wise men, conjurers, magicians, [nor] diviners are able to declare [it] to the king.

28 "However, there is a God in heaven who reveals mysteries, and He has made known to King Nebuchadnezzar what will take place in the latter days. This was your dream and the visions in your mind [while] on your bod.

29 "As for you, O king, [while] on your bed your thoughts turned to what would take place in the future; and He who reveals mysteries has made known to you what will take place.

30 "But as for me, this mystery has not been revealed to me for any wisdom residing in me more than [in] any [other] living man, but for the purpose of making the interpretation known to the king, and that you may understand the thoughts of your mind.

31 "You, O king, were looking and behold, there was a single great statue; that statue, which was large and of extraordinary splendor, was standing in front of you, and its appearance was awesome.

32 "The head of that statue [was made] of fine gold, its breast and its arms of silver, its belly and its thighs of bronze,

33 its legs of iron, its feet partly of iron and partly of clay.

34 "You continued looking until a stone was cut out without hands, and it struck the statue on its feet of iron and clay, and crushed them.

35 "Then the iron, the clay, the bronze, the silver and the gold were crushed all at the same time, and became like chaff from the summer threshing floors; and the wind carried them away so that not a trace of them was found. But the stone that struck the statue became a great mountain and filled the whole earth.

36 "This [was] the dream; now we shall tell its interpretation before the king.

37 "You, O king, are the king of kings, to whom the God of heaven has given the kingdom, the power, the strength, and the glory;

38 and wherever the sons of men dwell, [or] the beasts of the field, or the birds of the sky, He has given [them] into your hand and has caused you to rule over them all. You are the head of gold.

39 "And after you there will arise another kingdom inferior to you, then another third kingdom of bronze, which will rule over all the earth.

40 "Then there will be a fourth kingdom as strong as iron; inasmuch as iron crushes and shatters all things, so, like iron that breaks in pieces, it will crush and break all these in pieces.

41 "And in that you saw the feet and toes, partly of potter's clay and partly of iron, it will be a divided kingdom; but it will have in it the toughness of iron, inasmuch as you saw the iron mixed with common clay.

42 "And [as] the toes of the feet [were] partly of iron and partly of pottery, [so] some of the kingdom will be strong and part of it will be brittle.

43 "And in that you saw the iron mixed with common clay, they will combine with one another in the seed of men; but they will not adhere to one another, even as iron does not combine with pottery.

44 "And in the days of those kings the God of heaven will set up a kingdom which will never be destroyed, and [that] kingdom will not be left for another people; it will crush and put an end to all these kingdoms, but it will itself endure forever.

45 "Inasmuch as you saw that a stone was cut out of the mountain without hands and that it crushed the iron, the bronze, the clay, the silver, and the gold, the great God has made known to the king what will take place in the future; so the dream is true, and its interpretation is trustworthy."

46 Then King Nebuchadnezzar fell on his face and did homage to Daniel, and gave orders to present to him an offering and fragrant incense.

47 The king answered Daniel and said, "Surely your God is a God of gods and a Lord of kings and a revealer of mysteries, since you have been able to reveal this mystery."

48 Then the king promoted Daniel and gave him many great gifts, and he made him ruler over the whole province of Babylon and chief prefect over all the wise men of Babylon.

40 And Daniel made request of the king, and he appointed Shadrach, Meshach and Abed-nego over the administration of the province of Babylon, while Daniel [was] at the king's court.

Daniel 3

1 Nebuchadnezzar the king made an image of gold, the height of which [was] sixty cubits [and] its width six cubits; he set it up on the plain of Dura in the province of Babylon.

2 Then Nebuchadnezzar the king sent [word] to assemble the satraps, the prefects and the governors, the counselors, the treasurers, the judges, the magistrates and all the rulers of the provinces to come to the dedication of the image that Nebuchadnezzar the king had set up.

3 Then the satraps, the prefects and the governors, the counselors, the treasurers, the judges, the magistrates and all the rulers of the provinces were assembled for the dedication of the image that Nebuchadnezzar the king had set up; and they stood before the image that Nebuchadnezzar had set up.

4 Then the herald loudly proclaimed: "To you the command is given, O peoples, nations and [men of every] language,

5 that at the moment you hear the sound of the horn, flute, lyre, trigon, psaltery, bagpipe, and all kinds of music, you are to fall down and worship the golden image that Nebuchadnezzar the king has set up.

6 "But whoever does not fall down and worship shall immediately be cast into the midst of a furnace of blazing fire."

7 Therefore at that time, when all the peoples heard the sound of the horn, flute, lyre, trigon, psaltery, bagpipe, and all kinds of music, all the peoples, nations and [men of every] language fell down [and] worshiped the golden image that Nebuchadnezzar the king had set up.

8 For this reason at that time certain Chaldeans came forward and brought charges against the Jews.

9 They responded and said to Nebuchadnezzar the king: "O king, live forever!

10 "You yourself, O king, have made a decree that every man who hears the sound of the horn, flute, lyre, trigon, psaltery, and bagpipe, and all kinds of music, is to fall down and worship the golden image.

11 "But whoever does not fall down and worship shall be cast into the midst of a furnace of blazing fire.

12 "There are certain Jews whom you have appointed over the administration of the province of Babylon, [namely] Shadrach, Meshach and Abed-nego. These men, O king, have disregarded you; they do not serve your gods or worship the golden image which you have set up."

13 Then Nebuchadnezzar in rage and anger gave orders to bring Shadrach, Meshach and Abed-nego; then these men were brought before the king.

14 Nebuchadnezzar responded and said to them, "Is it true, Shadrach, Meshach and Abed-nego, that you do not serve my gods or worship the golden image that I have set up?

15 "Now if you are ready, at the moment you hear the sound of the horn, flute, lyre, trigon, psaltery, and bagpipe, and all kinds of music, to fall down and worship the image that I have made, [very well.] But if you will not worship, you will immediately be cast into the midst of a furnace of blazing fire; and what god is there who can deliver you out of my hands?"

16 Shadrach, Meshach and Abed-nego answered and said to the king, "O Nebuchadnezzar, we do not need to give you an answer concerning this matter.

17 "If it be [so,] our God whom we serve is able to deliver us from the furnace of blazing fire; and He will deliver us out of your hand, O king.

18 "But [even] if [He does] not, let it be known to you, O king, that we are not going to serve your gods or worship the golden image that you have set up."

19 Then Nebuchadnezzar was filled with wrath, and his facial expression was altered toward Shadrach, Meshach and Abed-nego. He answered by

giving orders to heat the furnace seven times more than it was usually heated.

20 And he commanded certain valiant warriors who [were] in his army to tie up Shadrach, Meshach and Abed-nego, in order to cast [them] into the furnace of blazing fire.

21 Then these men were tied up in their trousers, their coats, their caps and their [other] clothes, and were cast into the midst of the furnace of blazing fire.

22 For this reason, because the king's command [was] urgent and the furnace had been made extremely hot, the flame of the fire slew those men who carried up Shadrach, Meshach and Abed-nego.

23 But these three men, Shadrach, Meshach and Abed-nego, fell into the midst of the furnace of blazing fire [still] tied up.

24 Then Nebuchadnezzar the king was astounded and stood up in haste; he responded and said to his high officials, "Was it not three men we cast bound into the midst of the fire?" They answered and said to the king, "Certainly, O king."

25 He answered and said, "Look! I see four men loosed [and] walking [about] in the midst of the fire without harm, and the appearance of the fourth is like a son of [the] gods!"

26 Then Nebuchadnezzar came near to the door of the furnace of blazing fire; he responded and said, "Shadrach, Meshach and Abed-nego, come out, you servants of the Most High God, and come here!" Then Shadrach, Meshach and Abed-nego came out of the midst of the fire.

27 And the satraps, the prefects, the governors and the king's high officials gathered around [and] saw in regard to these men that the fire had no effect on the bodies of these men nor was the hair of their head singed, nor were their trousers damaged, nor had the smell of fire [even] come upon them.

28 Nebuchadnezzar responded and said, "Blessed be the God of Shadrach, Meshach and Abed-nego, who has sent His angel and delivered His servants who put their trust in Him, violating the king's command, and yielded up their bodies so as not to serve or worship any god except their own God.

29 "Therefore, I make a decree that any people, nation or tongue that speaks anything offensive against the God of Shadrach, Meshach and Abed-nego shall be torn limb from limb and their houses reduced to a rubbish heap, inasmuch as there is no other god who is able to deliver in this way."

30 Then the king caused Shadrach, Meshach and Abed-nego to prosper in the province of Babylon.

Daniel 4

4:1 Nebuchadnezzar the king to all the peoples, nations, and [men of every] language that live in all the earth: "May your peace abound!

2 "It has seemed good to me to declare the signs and wonders which the Most High God has done for me.

3 "How great are His signs, And how mighty are His wonders! His kingdom is an everlasting kingdom, And His dominion is from generation to generation.

4 "I, Nebuchadnezzar, was at ease in my house and flourishing in my palace.

5 "I saw a dream and it made me fearful; and [these] fantasies [as I lay] on my bed and the visions in my mind kept alarming me.

6 "So I gave orders to bring into my presence all the wise men of Babylon, that they might make known to me the interpretation of the dream.

7 "Then the magicians, the conjurers, the Chaldeans, and the diviners came in, and I related the dream to them; but they could not make its interpretation known to me.

8 "But finally Daniel came in before me, whose name is Belteshazzar according to the name of my god, and in whom is a spirit of the holy gods; and I related the dream to him, [saying,]

9 'O Belteshazzar, chief of the magicians, since I know that a spirit of the holy gods is in you and no mystery baffles you, tell [me] the visions of my dream which I have seen, along with its interpretation.

10 'Now [these were] the visions in my mind [as I lay] on my bed: I was looking, and behold, [there was] a tree in the midst of the earth, and its height [was] great.

11 'The tree grew large and became strong, And its height reached to the sky, And it [was] visible to the end of the whole earth.

12 'Its foliage [was] beautiful and its fruit abundant, And in it [was] food for all. The beasts of the field found shade under it, And the birds of the

sky dwelt in its branches, And all living creatures fed themselves from it.

13 'I was looking in the visions in my mind [as I lay] on my bed, and behold, an [angelic] watcher, a holy one, descended from heaven.

14 'He shouted out and spoke as follows:

"Chop down the tree and cut off its branches, Strip off its foliage and scatter its fruit; Let the beasts flee from under it, And the birds from its branches.

15 "Yet leave the stump with its roots in the ground, But with a band of iron and bronze [around it] In the new grass of the field; And let him be drenched with the dew of heaven, And let him share with the beasts in the grass of the earth.

16 "Let his mind be changed from [that of] a man, And let a beast's mind be given to him, And let seven periods of time pass over him.

17 "This sentence is by the decree of the [angelic] watchers, And the decision is a command of the holy ones, In order that the living may know That the Most High is ruler over the realm of mankind, And bestows it on whom He wishes, And sets over it the lowliest of men."

18 'This is the dream [which] I, King Nebuchadnezzar, have seen. Now you, Belteshazzar, tell [me] its interpretation, inasmuch as none of the wise men of my kingdom is able to make known to me the interpretation; but you are able, for a spirit of the holy gods is in you.'

19 "Then Daniel, whose name is Belteshazzar, was appalled for a while as his thoughts alarmed him. The king responded and said, 'Belteshazzar, do not let the dream or its interpretation alarm you.' Belteshazzar answered and said, 'My lord, [if only] the dream applied to those who hate you, and its interpretation to your adversaries!

20 'The tree that you saw, which became large and grew strong, whose height reached to the sky and was visible to all the earth,

21 and whose foliage [was] beautiful and its fruit abundant, and in which [was] food for all, under which the beasts of the field dwelt and in whose branches the birds of the sky lodged--

22 it is you, O king; for you have become great and grown strong, and your majesty has become great and reached to the sky and your dominion to the end of the earth.

23 'And in that the king saw an [angelic] watcher, a holy one, descending from heaven and saying, "Chop down the tree and destroy it; yet leave the stump with its roots in the ground, but with a band of iron and bronze [around it] in the new grass of the field, and let him be drenched with the dew of heaven, and let him share with the beasts of the field until seven periods of time pass over him";

24 this is the interpretation, O king, and this is the decree of the Most High, which has come upon my lord the king:

25 that you be driven away from mankind, and your dwelling place be with the beasts of the field, and you be given grass to eat like cattle and be drenched with the dew of heaven; and seven periods of time will pass over you, until you recognize that the Most High is ruler over the realm of mankind, and bestows it on whomever He wishes.

26 'And in that it was commanded to leave the stump with the roots of the tree, your kingdom will be assured to you after you recognize that [it is] Heaven [that] rules.

27 'Therefore, O king, may my advice be pleasing to you: break away now from your sins by [doing] righteousness, and from your iniquities by showing mercy to [the] poor, in case there may be a prolonging of your prosperity.'

28 "All [this] happened to Nebuchadnezzar the king.

29 "Twelve months later he was walking on the [roof of] the royal palace of Babylon.

30 "The king reflected and said, 'Is this not Babylon the great, which I myself have built as a royal residence by the might of my power and for the glory of my majesty?'

31 "While the word [was] in the king's mouth, a voice came from heaven, [saying,] 'King Nebuchadnezzar, to you it is declared: sovereignty has been removed from you,

32 and you will be driven away from mankind, and your dwelling place [will be] with the beasts of the field. You will be given grass to eat like cattle, and seven periods of time will pass over you, until you recognize that the Most High is ruler over the realm of mankind, and bestows it on whomever He wishes.'

33 "Immediately the word concerning Nebuchadnezzar was fulfilled; and he was driven away from mankind and began eating grass like cattle, and his body was drenched with the dew of heaven, until his hair had grown like eagles' [feathers] and his nails like birds' [claws].

34 "But at the end of that period I, Nebuchadnezzar, raised my eyes toward heaven, and my reason returned to me, and I blessed the Most High and praised and honored Him who lives forever;

For His dominion is an everlasting dominion, And His kingdom [endures] from generation to generation.

35 "And all the inhabitants of the earth are accounted as nothing, But He does according to His will in the host of heaven And [among] the inhabitants of earth; And no one can ward off His hand Or say to Him, 'What hast Thou done?'

36 "At that time my reason returned to me. And my majesty and splendor were restored to me for the glory of my kingdom, and my counselors and my nobles began seeking me out; so I was reestablished in my sovereignty, and surpassing greatness was added to me.

37 "Now I Nebuchadnezzar praise, exalt, and honor the King of heaven, for all His works are true and His ways just, and He is able to humble those who walk in pride."

Lesson Two

If you were to read the mythologies of all cultures, you would find creation myths, flood myths, and many stories that are very similar to the tower of Babel account found in Genesis. Many people say that the presence of these stories in all cultures simply proves that the Biblical account is merely one of many creation/flood/Babel myths...and if we would be honest about our interpretations of these Hebrew myths we would not give them any more credibility that we give those of all the other cultures —these are just primitive man's primitive attempts to explain his origins and existence to his primitive self.

Others say that the presence of these stories in all cultures obviously proves that these stories had a common origin in actual historical events——a historical creation, a historical Tower of Babel and a historic world-wide flood.

How would you argue?

The Epic of Gilgamesh is a Babylonian poem that includes a Babylonian flood story that has quite a bit in common with the Genesis account of the Flood. This poem is the first piece of non-Biblical ancient literature that you are going to study. By the time you finish studying it, you should be familiar enough with both the Genesis account and *The Epic of Gilgamesh* account to be prepared to argue your position with conviction.

The Gilgamesh named in this epic, is the King Gilgamesh whose name is listed on the Sumerian Kings List as the fifth king to have ruled after the Flood. For obvious reasons, this list is usually not considered to be a historically factual record, but it is useful to look at it just to note that there was a King Gilgamesh listed, and to see where in the sequence of kings his name appears.

Sumerian King List

In Eanna, **Meskiaggasher,** the son of the Utu (the sun god)
Reigned as priest and king for 324 years –
Meskiaggasher entered the sea, ascended the
mountains.
Enmerkar, the son of Meskaggasher, the king of Erech
Who had built Erech, reigned 420 years as king.
Lugalbanda, the shepherd, reigned 1,200 years.
Dumuzi, the fisherman, whose city was Dua, reigned 100
years.
Gilgamesh, whose father was a nomad, reigned 126 years.
Meshede reigned 30 years.
Labasher reigned 9 years.
Ennundaranna reigned 8 years.
Meshede reigned 36 years.
Melamanna reigned 6 years.
Lugalkidul reigned 36 years.

Total: twelve kings, reigned 2,120 years. Erech was defeated, its kingship was carried off to Ur.

The list describes three periods. The first period began "after the kingship descended from heaven [when] Eridu became the seat of kingship." This period involves five cities, eight kings, and lasted 241,200 years. After this period, the *List* says, "The Flood then swept over." And Kish becomes the seat of Kingship. After Kish was defeated, Eanna became the new seat of Kingship.

The dates for Gilgamesh's reign in Uruk are generally assumed to be about 2650 B.C. By about 1800 B.C., *The Epic of Gilgamesh* had appeared in a reasonably standard form. Daniel first arrived in Babylon between 600 and 500 B.C. Therefore, it is very reasonable to assume that *Gilgamesh* would have been included in the "language and literature of the Chaldeans" mentioned in Daniel 1. Daniel would also have read and studied this story of Gilgamesh.

But before *you* begin reading *The Epic of Gilgamesh*, I want you to be very familiar with the Biblical accounts of Creation, Babel, the Flood and the men who were eyewitnesses of each of those events, so that you (like Daniel before you) will begin your study of Babylonian material with a solid understanding of the Genesis accounts.

Therefore, you are going to spend quite a bit of time with the most exciting (and most often skimmed) verses in Genesis as you make a quick overview of the book of "Beginnings.

DAY ONE

Read Genesis chapters 1-3.

Answer the following questions:
Chapter 1

1. What do you learn about what kind of God the God of Genesis is, just from reading chapter 1?

2. How does he create?

3. What does he seem to be most concerned with?

4. Does this God seem primitive or sophisticated?

Chapters 2-3

1. Describe God's relationship with the man.

2. Where does God put the garden? Why so specific?

Skim through the rest of Genesis. Stop at the following places and notice the phrases repeated at each place. Write each phrase out below next to the reference.

Gen. 5.1

Gen. 6.9

Gen. 10.1

Gen. 11.10

Gen. 11.27

Gen. 36.1

Gen. 37.1

What does this phrase tell us about the sources Moses used in writing the book of Genesis?

DAY TWO

1. Read Genesis 4-5

What do these two chapters tell us about early man? To answer this, we are going to spend a lot of time in the genealogies found in these two chapters.

Fill out the genealogy charts for Adam and his two oldest sons. Obviously Abel leaves no children, so chart Cain's seed.

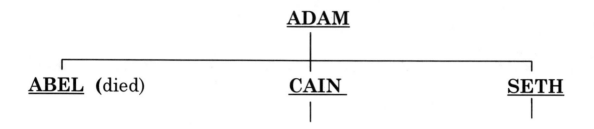

2. What is the first thing Cain does?

3. How long (how many generations) before some men begin to live nomadically? What else is happening at the same time?

4. Compare the sequence of these events with the sequence typically given in an evolution-based sequence of how early man developed. What kinds of things does early man do first? What types of things come later? (This is going to involve some research. Refer to encyclopedias, Usborne books, etc. and make notes on what you find here.)

DAY THREE

1. Complete the "Talk to an Eyewitness Genealogy Chart" (page 44) through Noah.

2. Find out who was alive when Adam was alive. When Seth was alive. How long would it have been possible to interview an eyewitness of the events of Genesis 2 and 3?

3. Trivia Question. What was the age difference between Shem, Ham, and Japheth?

Talk to an Eyewitness Genealogy Chart

Major Event	Years from Creation born		More years lived	year died	
Creation	0	became a **Adam** father at - (130)	800	930	
	130	**Seth** ( )			
		Enosh ( )			
		Kenan ( )			
		Mahalel ( )			
		Jared ( )			
		Enoch ( )			
		Methuselah ( )			--Name means: *After me it cimes*
		Lamech ( )			
		Noah ( )			
Shem Ham Japheth		Japheth Shem Ham ( )			(When Noah is 600 years old)
FLOOD		Arpachshad ( )			--Shem's line
		Salah ( )			
		Eber ( )			
Babel		Peleg ( )			Genesis 10:25
		Reu ( )			
		Serug ( )			
		Nahor ( )			
		Terah ( )			
		Abram ( )			
		Isaac ( )Gen.25.26	Gen.35.28		
		Jacob ( )			
		Joseph ( )		Gen.50.22	

In whose lifetime did these men die: Adam, Seth, Noah, Shem, Peleg?

DAY FOUR

Read Genesis 6: 1—9:29.

1. How is the condition of man described in Genesis 6?

2. How does God respond to it?

3. Why does God decide to do away with mankind?

4. Why does he decide to spare Noah?

5. How old was Noah when the flood waters came?

6. How long did the flooding last?

7. What is God's relationship with Noah? With the beasts?

8. What kinds of things is God concerned with? What does that tell us about His character?

Genesis 10

9. Where do Japheth's children settle?

10. Where do Ham's children settle (especially Cush and Nimrod)?

DAY FIVE

Genesis 11:1-9

1. Who is mentioned in this section?

2. Where are they?

3. Who in chapter 10 was associated with this region?

4. What do they want to do? Why do they want to do this?
   (Some people have seen a connection between this and Genesis 6.4.
   What do you think?)

5. So what happened?

Genesis 11:10-26

**Fill out the rest of the "Talk to an Eyewitness Genealogy Chart."
(page 44).**

1. Who is alive when Noah dies?

2. Who is alive when Seth dies?

3. What happens during Peleg's life (Genesis 10.25)?

4. Who was alive when Peleg dies?

5. How long was an eyewitness to the flood alive? Through what person?

6. How long was an eyewitness to the tower of Babel alive? Though what person?

Good work! Treat yourself to something chocolate!

Hey MOM! My homework says I should go eat chocolate now.

Lesson Three
The Epic of Gilgamesh

Vocabulary:
(Note: This vocabulary list is taken from the Penguin Classics edition of *The Epic of Gilgamesh*,, translated by N.K. Sanders. If you are reading from another translation, you will need to make your own list.)

For each of the works you study, you will have a list of vocabulary words taken from the material assigned. Do not limit yourself to this list. If, as you read, you find a word you cannot define, look it up, too. If you do not understand what the words you are reading mean, you won't understand what you are reading....funny thing, huh?

I.   The Coming of Enkidu

toscin
resolute
lament
lurked
benumber
range (verb)
extol
rouse
throng (verb)
jostle
byre

II. The Forest Journey

foray
torrent
supplicate
quay
succor
rancour/rancor
pommel
hilt
abhor
exhortation
foundling

hierophants
votaries
amulet
scabbard
league
precipece
ominous
cower
execration

III. Ishtar and Gligamesh, and the Death of Enkidu

eminent
imminent
cubits
ferrule
jamb
wattle
obliterate
vile
fouled (hint: no one is playing baseball or basketball)
hovel
pelt (noun)
lapis lazuli
carnelian
sombre/somber
talon
vampire
incantation
ecstasy
bailiff
gazelle
hyena
whelps (noun)
strew
abomination

IV. The Search for Everlasting Life

pap
felon
allotted
bitumen
transit
larva

V. The Story of the Flood

abyss

VI. The Return

harbourage
sluices

VII. The Death of Gilgamesh

concubine

1. Read through the whole epic once to get a feel for the story. After you have finished reading through it, record your initial impressions of the following characters below

   Gilgamesh:

   Enkidu:

   the gods:

   Utnapishtim:

> *The Epic of Gilgamesh* is an example of **epic poetry.** In an epic poem, the hero often seems "larger than life," performing grand, amazing deeds. The hero represents or embodies the highest ideals and values of the culture. Guess what the hero of an epic poem is called? An **epic hero**, of course. (You're so smart!)
> (HINT: KNOW THIS!)

2. Now for the rest of the week, read through the epic more slowly.

   I.   The Coming of Enkidu, pp. 62-69
   II. The Forest Journey, pp. 70-84
   III. Ishtar and Gilgamesh, and the Death of Enkidu, pp. 85-96
   IV. The Search for Everlasting Life, pp. 97-107
   V.   The Story of the Flood, pp. 108-113
   VI. The Return, pp. 114-117
   VII. The Death of Gilgamesh, pp. 118-119

   Read each section **carefully** (do not skim). Look up any words you do not understand (even if that word is **not** on the vocabulary list at the beginning of this lesson!) and write the meaning in the margin of your book.

3. **As you finish each section**, record the following things on your "Gilgamesh Overview Chart," page 57-58.

   • The major character or characters you just read about in that section
   • The main thing that happened in that section only
   • Any general impressions, thoughts, questions, or quotations that seem to be significant

4. **As you read**, note Gilgamesh's attitudes toward the following:

   • the people he rules
   • death (or the thought of dying)
   • the gods in general
   • any particular god or goddess

   If you notice any changes in his attitudes toward any of these things, be sure and mark the place where you find that change in your text. Then record your observations on the chart titled, "Gilgamesh's Attitude Check!" found on pages 59-60.

5. Compare and contrast the character of the gods of Gilgamesh and the character of the God of Genesis. You may also refer back to the observations you made as you were studying the passages from Daniel. Are there any similarities between the two deities? How are they different? BE VERY SPECIFIC! Record your answers on the chart titled, "God and the Babylonian gods," page 61.

6. Review the Genesis account of the Flood beginning in Genesis 6. Using the chart labeled "Events in the Genesis Flood/Events in Gilgamesh Flood," page 62, record the key facts about each. How are the accounts similar? How are they different?

7. **Make sure you can answer the following questions.**
(Some of these questions could form the basis of some very good short essay assignments.)

Factual/observation Questions

A. Briefly identify the following characters:
    i. Gilgamesh
    ii. Enkidu
    iii. Humbaba
    iv. Ishtar
    v. the Bull of Heaven
    vi. Elil

B. What two things do Gilgamesh and his friend kill?

C. Tell what happens to Gilgamesh's friend. Why does this happen?

D. How does Gilgamesh react to his friend's fate?

E. Describe Gilgamesh's quest. Where does he go, and what does he seek?

F. Who is Siduri? What does she do? How does she advise Gilgamesh?

G. Who is Utnapishtim? Describe Gilgamesh's resolve to find eternal life.

H. How does Utnapishtim test Gilgamesh?

I. Upon returning home, what does Gilgamesh do? What is he like? Has he changed any? Explain your answers.

J. According to Utnapishtim, why did the gods once try to destroy mankind?

K. Discussion Questions:
   a. (Some of these questions could be explored in a longer essay.)

L. Compare and contrast the gods of *The Epic of Gilgamesh* with the God of the Bible. Be very specific and cite references to both the Bible and *The Epic of Gilgamesh* to support your answers. Merely saying, "The God of the Bible is real and the others are not," is not a sufficient answer.

M. Would you say that Gilgamesh changes as the story progresses? In what ways does he change or not change? What influences him?

N. Describe Gilgamesh's relationship with Ishtar. Compare that relationship with God's relationship with Adam or Noah.

O. Tell two ways in which the Gilgamesh flood account *could* be seen as evidence for the historical accuracy of the Genesis flood account.

P. Describe Gilgamesh's relationship with the other gods. (Start by asking questions like these: What is the relationship like at the first of the poem? In what ways does the relationship grow? What do we learn about Gilgamesh as we observe him in this relationship? Is he changing? If so, how? If not, how?

Q. Describe Gilgamesh's relationship with Enkidu.

R. Describe Gilgamesh's attitude toward death.

S. What is the afterlife like according to the poem? Given the character of the gods as portrayed here, is the afterlife what you would expect? How? How not?

T. Compare this Sumerian view of the afterlife with that of the Bible. Make reference to specific Bible verses. "I don't know where it comes from, but I remember hearing in Sunday School one time" is not a sufficient source.

U. Describe Enkidu's attitude toward death. Compare it with Gilgamesh's attitude toward death.

V. In what ways could you consider Gilgamesh an epic hero?

W. What other questions or issues occurred to you as you read that you would like to discuss or explore?

GILGAMESH OVERVIEW CHART

Section	Main Characters	Main Events	Comments
I			
II			
III			

GILGAMESH OVERVIEW CHART

Section	Main Characters	Main Events	Comments
IV			
V			
VI			
VII			

GILGAMESH'S ATTITUDE CHECK

Section	Toward subjects	Toward death	Toward deity
I			
II			
III			

GILGAMESH'S ATTITUDE CHECK

Section	Toward subjects	Toward death	Toward deity
IV			
V			
VI			
VII			

GOD and the Babylonian gods

God of Genesis/Daniel	gods of Gilgamesh
Be sure to cite references!	
General Character:	*General Character:*
Relationship with Creation:	*Relationship with Creation:*
Relationship with Mankind:	*Relationship with Mankind:*

Events in Genesis Flood	What verse?	In common yes/no?	Events in Gilgamesh Flood

Lesson Four
Comparisons between Genesis and Gilgamesh
(and some thoughts on presuppositions)

You have now carefully read the Genesis record of man's beginnings, and you have carefully read a Sumerian/Babylonian account of similar events. You should have made some detailed observations about the basic events described in each account and the nature of the deities involved. In **this** lesson you are ready to review those observations and begin to draw some conclusions based on them.

(SO, if you have done only a superficial job on Lesson 3, now would be an *excellent* time to go back and do it right!)

When people read the ancient writings, they draw conclusions about the nature of the events described in them. That is, they ask, "Is this true? Did it really happen? Did it really happen *this* way? Is there some kernel of truth in this?" They also draw some conclusions about the nature or character of early man.

Usually, a person will come to these texts with a certain set of *presuppositions*. **Presuppositions** are those things that you *assume* to be true at the beginning. They are the *positions* you suppose to be true before you look any further at an idea, a person, a place, or a thing. A person's presuppositions form the foundation of the way a person will look at everything around them.

If you *presuppose*, for example, that all four -year old children are deaf, how would you be likely to talk to one?

Some of you would be likely to start out by shouting. The more sophisticated among you might try some sign language. Your presupposition that all four-year old children are deaf would be tasted during that first encounter.

Maybe it would go something like this:

You (shouting):   HELLO, LITTLE KID!
Four year old (annoyed): I'm NOT DEAF!
                             Why are you SHOUTING AT ME?

At this point in your encounter, you would have three choices.

- You could either think, "Hmmm, I guess all four year olds aren't so deaf." (Discard the presupposition)
- Or you could think, "What's *wrong* with this four year old? He heard me! This one's amazing!" (Assume that this is an exception to the rule.)
- Or, because you **know** that **your** presupposition cannot possibly be wrong, you could ignore the obvious and continue shouting. (Hold to the presupposition despite contradictory evidence.)

Which would be the most logical response, do you think?

For every position, there will be some set of *presup*positions. If you understand an argument's presuppositions, you will understand the issues more clearly.

If we look at our friend who only seems to know how to shout at innocent children without understanding his presuppositions, we might draw a number of conclusions about him in attempt to understand his behavior.

- We might assume that he hates four year olds.
- We might assume that he has some hearing problem himself and doesn't realize that he is shouting.
- We might assume that he has some mental problem.

If we assume that he hates four year olds, we might try to talk to him about how wonderful four year olds are. If we assume that he has some hearing or mental problem, we might try to convince him to get help for his condition. None of these arguments would be likely to stop the shouting, because none address the real reason he is shouting.

To stop him from shouting, we would have to deal with his underlying assumptions about four year old children.

In the same way, a person's own presuppositions about the origin of man will affect the way he or she interprets the Genesis and Sumerian flood accounts.

If a person presupposes that Evolution accurately describes the origins of mankind, they will likely draw one set of conclusions. If they have presupposed that the Bible is inspired by God, accurate, and infallible, they will be likely to draw another set of conclusions.

In this lesson, you are going to continue making some observations about the nature of these two floods.

Basic presuppositions of an evolutionary worldview usually assume the following to be true.

- Life began as the simplest of forms (single cell) and gradually evolved into more complex forms.
- This was a natural process that did not require any supernatural intervention. Though it is possible to believe that something supernatural actually started the process, it is also possible to explain life's beginnings by way of some random natural event.
- This is a pattern (simple to complex) all life follows as it continues to evolve toward the perfected state.

To find the basic presuppositions of a Biblical view of the history of man, you are going to do a close inductive study of Romans 1:16-32. A copy of this section of Romans is included on the following pages for you to mark. You will also need a pen, a green pencil, and a red pencil. Just follow the directions given below.

1. Read through the passage slowly and carefully. Do not skim.
2. WHO is mentioned in the passage? List the different people (really *types* of people) mentioned.

3. Mark all references to *righteous man* or *men* (or any pronouns that refer to these men) in **green.**
4. Mark all references to *unrighteous man* or *men* (or any pronouns that refer to them) in **red.**
5. List the things all men can know about God in the margin of your worksheet.
6. Even though, as verse 21 says, men KNEW God, what does it say they did with that knowledge? List these things:

7. Circle the word *exchanged* each time you see it.
8. List the things that were exchanged. What were they exchanged *for*?

9. Underline the phrase *God gave them over*. Do you see a progression involved here? (One thing leading to another thing...)

10. What is the relationship between the exchanges and God's "giving them over?"

11. What does this passage teach about the development of man's religious beliefs? What did man believe first? How did his beliefs change?

12. From the reading you did on evolution earlier, what does an evolutionary perspective say about the development of man's religion? What did man believe first? How did these beliefs change over time?

Romans 1:16-32

16 For I am not ashamed of the gospel of Christ: for it is the power of God unto salvation to every one that believeth; to the Jew first, and also to the Greek.

17 For therein is the righteousness of God revealed from faith to faith: as it is written, The just shall live by faith.

18 For the wrath of God is revealed from heaven against all ungodliness and unrighteousness of men, who hold the truth in unrighteousness;

19 Because that which may be known of God is manifest in them; for God hath shewed it unto them.

20 For the invisible things of him from the creation of the world are clearly seen, being understood by the things that are made, even his eternal power and Godhead; so that they are without excuse:

21 Because that, when they knew God, they glorified him not as God, neither were thankful; but became vain in their imaginations, and their foolish heart was darkened.

22 Professing themselves to be wise, they became fools,

23 And changed the glory of the uncorruptible God into an image made like to corruptible man, and to birds, and fourfooted beasts, and creeping things.

24 Wherefore God also gave them up to uncleanness through the lusts of their own hearts, to dishonour their own bodies between themselves:

25 Who changed the truth of God into a lie, and worshipped and served the creature more than the Creator, who is blessed for ever. Amen.

26 For this cause God gave them up unto vile affections: for even their women did change the natural use into that which is against nature:

27 And likewise also the men, leaving the natural use of the woman, burned in their lust one toward another; men with men working that which is unseemly, and receiving in themselves that recompence of their error which was meet.

28 And even as they did not like to retain God in their knowledge, God gave them over to a reprobate mind, to do those things which are not convenient;

29 Being filled with all unrighteousness, fornication, wickedness, covetousness, maliciousness; full of envy, murder, debate, deceit, malignity; whisperers,

30 Backbiters, haters of God, despiteful, proud, boasters, inventors of evil things, disobedient to parents,

31 Without understanding, covenantbreakers, without natural affection, implacable, unmerciful:

32 Who knowing the judgment of God, that they which commit such things are worthy of death, not only do the same, but have pleasure in them that do them.

13. Compare and contrast the two views of man presented in this passage of Romans and in an evolutionary view.

QUICK SUMMARY/REVIEW

The typical evolutionary view holds that primitive man began by superstitiously worshipping everything (animism) and then gradually progressed to more and more sophisticated concepts of deity (polytheism, monotheism). How does this view compare with the sequence Paul describes in Romans 1. Can both be historically true?

---

14. Review your observations about Cain and his descendants. According to the Genesis account, what did early man do first? List these things in order of appearance.

15. How does the Genesis account of early man's social and technological development compare with a typical evolutionary scenario?

16. If a person has an evolutionary worldview, would they be more likely to say that the Genesis account was written before or after *The Epic of Gilgamesh*? Explain your answer.

17. How would a person with a Biblical worldview be likely to date the two accounts? Explain your answer.

18. Which do **you** believe to be accurate? Why?

19. We know from Daniel, that Nebuchadnezzar interviewed Daniel and his friends after they completed their studies. Although we don't know what they talked about in that interview, we do know that *The Epic of Gilgamesh* would have been a part of Chaldean literature at that time. So . . . if Daniel and his friends had talked with Nebuchadnezzar about *The Epic of Gilgamesh* – what could they have told him?

20. As a final Gilgamesh assignment, do one of the following:

   - You are one of the four young Hebrews. Write Nebuchadnezzar a letter about *The Epic of Gilgamesh*. What would you tell him? (Remember when he reads it he should be impressed with your diligence and scholarship.)
   - Write a script of a conversation between the four Hebrew youths and Nebuchadnezzar. What would his questions be? How would the youths answer? Let the personalities of the four men come through! Have fun!

Lesson Five
The Odyssey
Chapters I-VI

If you are familiar with some of the history of Ancient Greece, know something about its mythology, or have even read a children's version of The Odyssey before, you may find that it helps you as you begin reading The Odyssey in translation. However, if all of this is new to you, don't worry. Even those who have studied some of this before will probably need a little review.

1. Study the following list of gods, goddesses, and mythological creatures. You need to know who these folks are before you begin *The Odyssey*, itself. You might want to get a copy of Edith Hamilton's *Mythology* and read a little about each of the personalities on the list. Knowing the stories that go with the entries will help you remember these things.

   Aeolus - god of the winds
   Athena - goddess of wisdom, science and the arts. Sprang full-formed and fully armored from the head of Zeus
   Calypso - enchantress who kept Odysseus on her island for seven years. Promised him eternal youth if he'd stay with her.
   Charybdis - monster, who with Scylla, destroyed ships
   Circe - enchantress who turned Odysseus' men into swine
   Hermes - messenger of the gods
   Hyperion - Titan father of Helios, Selene, and Eos. Early sun god who was the son of Uranus and Ge. Had sacred cattle.
   Leucothoie - sea goddess. As a mortal she was called Ioa, who hurled herself into the ocean in order to escape her husband. The gods changed her into a goddess.
   Polyphemus – one of the Cyclops
   Poseidon - god of the sea
   Scylla - Charybdis's monster partner in aquatic mayhem!
   The Sirens - beautiful sea maidens whose lovely songs maddened sailors who would crash their ships on the rocks trying to get closer.
   Zeus - king of the gods

2. Find out everything you can about Homer (He's the author of the Odyssey.) Who was he? Where did he live? What did he do and so on. Write a short summary of the information you find. (How long is "short" is up to your teacher.)

> *The Odyssey* is another example of **epic poetry.** Epic poetry expresses the highest ideals and values of a culture. The **epic hero** embodies and represents the culture's picture of the ideals of virtues and heroism.
> (HINT: MAKE SURE YOU KNOW THIS!)

3. **Vocabulary: Be able to define.**

harried
plundered
nymph
ordain
regaled
patrimony
beguiling
baleful
buffets
relent
flouting
ambrosial
haft
retainers
irk(ed)
din
larder
adept
spurn

4. **Read Chapter 1 of *The Odyssey*.**
   As you read, make notes on your OVERVIEW WORKSHEETS beginning on page 81, write the answers to the following questions on the worksheet charts in the spaces provided for the first chapter.

- **WHO are the main actors in each chapter?**
  Just record the MAIN personalities. If several of the suitors are involved in the same activity, just identify them as "the suitors."

- **Briefly summarize the main actions/events of the chapter.**
  Again, remember this is an *overview*. Keep it short and simple. Note the MAIN activities described in each chapter.

  Example (of sorts):
  Arthur storms the castle. Defenders yell at Arthur. Arthur threatens to attack. Defenders throw large chunks of beef over the wall at Arthur.

Do not feel the need to supply a word for word, action for action, "he-said-then-she-said" description. This is just to help you think through what you have read so that you will be able to remember what you have read.

- **If there are lines that you particularly liked or seem to be significant, you can write them down in the comment column.**

  Or, if something in the chapter really strikes you, write that in the comment column. Use the comment column to note any impressions of, or reactions to the things you are reading.

ODYSSEY OVERVIEW WORKSHEETS

Chap.#	WHO	WHAT HAPPENS	COMMENTS
1			
2			
3			
4			

Ch #	WHO	WHAT HAPPENS	COMMENTS
5			
6			
7			
8			

Ch #	WHO	WHAT HAPPENS	COMMENTS
9			
10			
11			
12			

Ch #	WHO	WHAT HAPPENS	COMMENTS
13			
14			
15			
16			

Ch #	WHO	WHAT HAPPENS	COMMENTS
17			
18			
19			
20			

The Greenleaf Guide to Ancient Literature

Ch #	WHO	WHAT HAPPENS	COMMENTS
21			
22			
23			
24			

5. In lines 42-62 of Chapter I, Homer describes Zeus meditating over the fate of Aigisthos "dead by the hand of Agamemnon's son, Orestes." This refers to the story of Agamemnon, the Greek general who was the "commander in chief" at Troy. Though he returned home, he didn't enjoy himself for very long. Read the rest of the story and find out why:

Aigisthos, Agamemnon and Clytemnestra

Just as Agamemnon's ships had been ready to sail for Troy, a terrible story blew up. Sure that the gods were angry with the Greeks, Agamemnon consulted a soothsayer named Calchas. Calchas told him that Artemis was angry with Agamemnon, himself. It seems that the last time Agamemnon had gone hunting he had killed a deer and boasted that he had greater skill than even Artemis, herself. Calchas told him that the storm would never be stilled until he offered his own daughter, Iphigenia as a sacrifice to the goddess.

Knowing that his wife, Klytaimnestra would never go for the idea, Agamemnon sent word that Achilles, another general, wanted to marry the girl, and asked her to send her to them at once. Mom did, expecting that her daughter would soon be the wife of the brave Achilles.

When Iphigenia arrived, Agamemnon explained the situation. Her answer to her father was, "If my death will help the Greeks, I am ready to die." So (in one version of the story) as she was lying on the altar, Artemis was moved to pity, and rescued the girl just before her father's sword fell, leaving a white fawn to be sacrificed in her place. Iphigenia was carried by the Artemis to one of her temples, where the girl as a priestess for the rest of her life. The storm stopped, and

the ships sailed for Troy. (In another
version of the story, she dies.)

Mom, however, was not happy with
either ending! Her love for Agamemnon was
dead and she wanted revenge. While he
was away at war, she fell in love with a
man named Aigisthos. To get even with
Agamemnon for taking Iphigenia from her,
she and Aigisthos made plans to kill him
when he returned.

When Agamemnon arrived, she fed
him a wonderful meal and served him the
finest of their wine. Then she suggested
that he take a long, relaxing bath before
going to bed. As she "helped" him take off
his shirt, she actually tangled him up in it.
As he was tangled in his shirt, Aigisthos
jumped from his hiding place and stabbed
him to death.

What neither of them had counted on, was
Agamemnon's son Orestes. Orestes took
vengeance on both of them, killing them
both for killing his father. A typical, loving
Greek family. The family that slays
together...as the saying goes. (Never mind.)

This is the story Zeus is pondering when Athena comes to
him on behalf of Odysseus. It is referred to and retold many
times throughout the poem. You get to figure out why.

6. Read Chapter I, pages 1-15. Fill out the Overview Chart for
   the chapter. As you read, make notes in the margin of your
   book briefly describing the main action of a section. This
   will help you focus your attention as you read.

Sometimes when you are first starting to read a long work of
poetry, you will tend to sort of fade in and out of
"consciousness." Your eyes keep moving over the page, but
you have no idea what you have just read. If this happens to
you, stop. Go back to the last section you remember

understanding (even if that was the title of the book...), and read one stanza.

As you read that one stanza, ask yourself the "who, what, when, where, why, how" questions. WHO is this section about? WHAT is he doing? WHERE is he? And so on. Make a note in the margin beside that stanza that very briefly describes the things that it describes or tells you.

Eventually, you will have trained yourself how to pay attention, and it will not seem so difficult.

7. Write (from memory) the main events of this first chapter. (If you can't do it, read the chapter again!)

8. Vocabulary: Define these words.

primal
sage
restitution
audacity
warp
rapine
vex(ing)
dowry
amphorai
laden
libation
prow

8. Read Chapter II, pages 19-31.

9. Fill out the **Overview Chart** for Chapter II. Remember to take notes as you read.

10. Write (from memory) the main events of this chapter.

11. What are your first impressions of the following people?

Athena

Penelope

Telemachus

The suitors

12. Vocabulary
brazen
precedence
harangued
astern

13. Read Chapter III, pages 35-49.

14. Fill out the **Overview Chart**.

15. Write the main events in Chapter III from memory.

16. Why does Homer repeat the story of Agamemnon's homecoming? What connection is there between his and Odysseus' story?

17. How is Athena's relationship with Odysseus described?

18. **Vocabulary**
    scion
    lithe
    equerries
    savories
    anodyne
    quested
    Nereid
    feign
    trident
    promontory
    squall
    galingale
    hoary
    abhor(red)
    forfend
    numinous

19. **Read Chapter IV, pages 53-78.**

20. Fill out the Overview Chart for Chapter IV.

21. So, who is the "red haired king," and who is his lady?

22. Write from memory the main events described in Chapter IV.

23. At line 668, the scene shifts from Menelaus's house back to where? Describe the action there.

24. What kind of homecoming do the suitors want to prepare for him?

25. **Vocabulary**
    sojourning
    cormorants
    peevish
    versatile
    puncheons
    ballast(ed)
    rondure
    perplexity
    traverse
    landspit
    estuary

26. **Read Chapter V, pages 81-95.**

27. Fill out the **Overview Chart** for Chapter V.

28. In lines 1- 47, who speaks?

    Describe Hermes's mission.

29. In lines 48-155, who speaks?

30. In lines 156-278, what happens?

31. In lines 179-291, what does Odysseus do?

32. In lines 292-307, who comes home, and what does he do?

33. In lines 308-389 who takes pity on Odysseus. Describe Odysseus' actions.

34. In lines 390-404, describe the actions of Poseidon (Earthshaker) and Athena.

35. In lines 405 through the end of the chapter, describe what happens.

36. Now write a summary of the events described in Chapter V.

37. **Vocabulary Define these words.**

    remiss
    brine
    megaron

38. **Read Chapter VI, pages 99-108.**

39. Fill out the **Overview Chart** for Chapter VI.

40. Write a summary of the action of Chapter VI from memory.

41. What are your first impressions of Odysseus? What kind of person does he seem to be?

42. What would you say are Odysseus' strengths? His weaknesses?

43. Describe his relationship with Athena. (Expect to be asked this question again as you read further in the poem.)

44. Is there anything that you are confused by so far? Describe your confusion here. Primal screams are acceptable, if followed by written explanation of scream. (Those who are occupying the house or the room with you, generally also appreciate a little prior warning like, "Okay folks, I am going to scream quite primally now.")

Lesson Six
The Odyssey
Chapters VII-XII

1. **Vocabulary**
   palisades
   luminous
   azure
   libation
   larder
   festal
   hekatombs
   assent
   tactician
   consorts
   auspicious

2. **Read Chapter VII, pages 111-121.**

3. Fill out the **Overview Chart** for Chapter VII.

4. Identify the following:

   Nausikaa
   Eurymedousa
   Alkinoos
   Phaiakians
   Ekheneo
   Kalypso

5. When Odysseus first enters the city, how does Athena disguise herself? What does she tell Odysseus about the people who live in Phaiakia?

6. Describe Odysseus' entry into the hall. How is he received?

7. The genealogy of the King and his wife Arete:

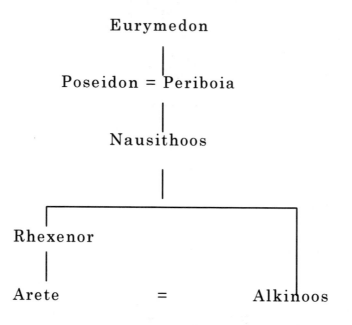

Eurymedon

Poseidon = Periboia

Nausithoos

Rhexenor

Arete   =   Alkinoos

So.... Rhexenor and Alkinoos are _____.

8. How is it that Alkinoos can claim that "we are their (the gods') kin; Gigantes, Kyklopes, rank no nearer gods than we?"

9. First Odysseus assures the Phaiakians that he is not a god, and that he is starving. Then he explains how he came to be wearing Arete's family's clothes. What does Alkinoos fault his daughter, Nausikaa, for not doing?

10. Finally, in this chapter, what does Odysseus ask of his hosts? How do they respond to his request?

11. **Vocabulary**

    tactician
    decorum

12. **Read Chapter VIII**, pages 125-142.

13. Fill out the **Overview Chart** for Chapter VIII.

14. Tell the main events in each of the following sections:

    Lines 1-25

    Lines 26-49

    Lines 50-77

    Lines 78-103

    Lines 104-138

    Lines 139-173

    Lines 174-245

    Lines 246-269

    Lines 270-396

Lines 397-411

Lines 412-475

Lines 476-487

Lines 488-500

Lines 501-532

Lines 533-574

Lines 575-626

15. Now summarize the main events/actions of this chapter.

16. **Vocabulary**
    boon
    formidable
    guile
    muster
    symmetrical
    prodigious
    avowal

17. **Read Chapter IX.**

18. In lines 1-40, Odysseus reveals his identity and his homeland, and then tells how he had been held by Kalypso against his will. He then says, "What of my sailing then, from Troy? What of those years of rough adventure, weathered under Zeus?" At this point, Odysseus begins to tell his own story. Summarize the stories he tells about each of these main events.

    His sailing to Ismaros:

    The Lotus Eaters:

    The Island of Kyklopes:

19. **Vocabulary**
    brazen
    ramparts
    stint(ed)
    bilge
    withies
    foreboding

20. **Read Chapter X, 165-182.**

21. Fill out the **Overview Chart** for Chapter X.

22. Summarize each of the following stories:

How Aiolos aids Odysseus and how the gift is squandered

The island of Lamos

Kirke

23. Kirke sends Odysseus to inquire of the dead in Hades before he continues on his journey. Why? Who, in particular, is he to seek?

24. **Vocabulary**

assuage
lugger
pommel
exanimate
limpid
largesse
glut
bastion
havoc
calamitous
roustabout
pandemonium

25. **Read Chapter XI, pages 185-206.**

26. *Shades* are spirits of the dead who now live in Hades. Find out who Persephone is. How did she come to Hades?

27. How does Odysseus draw the shades to him?

28. In line 100 through line 167, Odysseus speaks with Teiresias. What does Teiresias tell him?

29. Who are the following, and what do they tell Odysseus?

    Elpenor

    Anticleia

30. From line 256 through line 381, what general group does Odysseus describe seeing?

31. From line 390 through line 412, what do Arete and Alkinoos propose? How does Odysseus respond?

32. In line 439, Odysseus takes up the story again. He begins with his encounter with Agamemnon. Describe that encounter.

33. Describe Odysseus' encounter with Akhilleus.

34. Describe the activities of the following:

Minos

Orion

Tityos

Tantalos

Sisyphos

Herakles

35. **Vocabulary**

hawsers
timorous
serried
maelstrom
blanched
comber

36. **Read Chapter XII, pages 209-225.**

37. Fill out the **Overview Chart** for Chapter XII.

38. In lines 1-170 Odysseus returns to Kirke's island. He fulfills his promise to Elpenor and listens to Kirke's descriptions of dangers that lie ahead of them. Who are the following, and what does Kirke say about each?

Seirenes (Sirens)

Skylla (Scylla)

Kharybdid (Charybdis)

Lord Helios cattle

39. Describe what happens as Odysseus and him men face each
    of these dangers:

    Seirenes (Sirens)

    Skylla (Scylla)

    Kharybdid (Charybdis)

    Lord Helios' cattle

40. Who ultimately destroys Odysseus' ship?

41. List the adjectives used to describes Odysseus throughout
    the chapters you have read so far.

42. What kind of man would you say Odysseus is? (Be detailed and give examples to support your descriptions. "A hungry man" is not a complete answer. "Odysseus proved himself hungry when he. . . " is a complete answer.)

43. Very specifically (based on what you have read so far), tell how Odysseus could be called an Epic Hero.

Lesson Seven
The Odyssey
Chapters XIII-XVIII

1. Vocabulary
> levy (make a levy upon the land to pay...)
> ardent
> benison
> felicity
> victual(ling)
> booty
> uncumbered (unencumbered)
> trove
> booby
> confiscation
> reimbark
> dissimulation
> chameleon
> contrive(r)
> gall
> wormwood
> hinterland
> cache
> crannies
> brazen
> forestall

2. **Read Chapter XIII, pages 229-244.**

3. Fill out the **Overview Chart** for Chapter XIII.

4. In lines 1-96, Odysseus leaves Phaiakia. Describe the send-off he is given.

5. Describe the action of lines 97-152.

6. Describe the conversation between Zeus and Poseidon in lines 153-235. What does Zeus allow Poseidon to do and not do? How do the Phaiakians respond?

7. In lines 236-551, we find Odysseus on Ithaka. For most of this section, he matches wits with Athena. What do they talk about?

8. What do you learn from these lines about Odysseus' relationship with Athena? Why does she favor him?

9. Odysseus realizes that he is likely to suffer the same fate as Agamemnon. "So hard beset! An end like Agamemnon's / might very well have been mine, a bad end / bleeding to death in my own hall." Who is Odysseus threatened by and how is this threat forestalled?

10. **Vocabulary**

   farrows
   carrion
   corsairs
   sojourn
   zenith
   petrels
   inveigled
   balsam

11. Fill out the **Overview Chart** for Chapter XIV.

12. Describe Eumaios. (Learn to spell his name so that you will recognize it when he appears later in the story. Otherwise, you will confuse him with the suitors later in the poem and be **really** confused.)

13. What kind of herd would a swineherd herd if a swineherd could herd swine?

14. How does Eumaios receive Odysseus?

15. Throughout this chapter Eumaios says many things about Zeus. Copy those passages out below. Write down line and page numbers so that you can find them in the book easily.

16. **VocabularyDefine these words.**

    portico
    clarion
    coffers
    nimble/nimbly

17. **Read Chapter XV, pages 267-286.**

18. Fill out the **Overview Chart** for Chapter XV.

19. How does Athena motivate Telemakhos to return home?

20. Describe the hospitality of Menelaos.

21. Notice how Telemakhos is described in this chapter. Write down the adjectives and phrases used to describe him.

22. Tell about the omen of the mountain eagle and the goose. How was it interpreted?

23. From line 373 to line 399, Odysseus tells Eumaios his plan to go to Odysseus' hall. In lines 400-417, how does Eumaios respond?

24. From line 418-463, what information does Eumaios give Odysseus about his wife and father?

25. How did the swineherd originally come to Ithaka?

26. **Vocabulary**

    quandary
    rancor
    ruddy
    oblation
    retainers
    shirker

27. **Read Chapter XVI, pages 289-305.**

28. Fill out the **Overview Chart** for Chapter XVI.

29. Describe the welcome Eumaios gives Telemakhos.

30. Eumaios introduces the disguised Odysseus to Telemakhos as a traveler who seeks his protection. How does Telemakhos respond?

31. In lines 109-130, why does Odysseus say these things to Telemakhos?

32. What does Telemakhos' answer (in lines 131-167) tell Odysseus?

33. Who appears in line 182 through 209, and what does she tell him? What does she do?

34. Describe Odysseus' reunion with his son.

35. Describe their plans for the suitors.

36. In lines 402-492, the sullen suitors respond to the news of Telemakhos' safe return. How **do** each of the following men respond?

      Amphinomos

      Atinoos

      Eurymakhos

37. Describe the conversation between Eurymakhos and Penelope. What insights do you gain into each of their characters?

38. What do Odysseus and Telemakhos learn from Eumaios on his return from town? Why doesn't Eumaios recognize Odysseus?

39. **Vocabulary**

    portent
    lop(ped)
    mendicant
    asset
    dire
    guise
    acclamation

40. **Read Chapter XVII, pages 309-331.**

41. Who is Melantios? How does he meet and treat Odysseus?

42. How does Odysseus go into his own hall? Who **does** recognize him?

43. How is Odysseus received?

44. Compare his reception here with the receptions he has received as he has entered other halls in previous chapters. Be specific.

45. Look for examples of **foreshadowing** as you read. **Foreshadowing** refers to places and situations within the story where the writer will hint at events or actions that will happen later in the story.

46. With question number 40 in mind, what is the significance of Telemakhos's sneeze? See lines 714-719.

47. Why does Odysseus delay a meeting with Penelope?

48. **Read Chapter XVIII, pages 335-350.**

49. Fill out the **Overview Chart** for Chapter XVIII.

50. Who is Arnaois/Iros? Describe Odysseus' interaction with him.

51. Why is it that Amphinomos does not heed Odysseus' warning?

52. Describe Penelope's appearance before the suitors. What does she say to Telemakhos?

53. Describe the conversation between Penelope and Eurymakhos. What do you learn about Euyrmakhos from it? What does Odysseus learn about Eurymakhos *and* Penelope from it?

54. Who is Melanthos? What do we learn about her? (BEWARE!! Do not confuse Melanthos with **Melanthios**)!

55. What does Odysseus learn about the housemaids?

56. Describe the encounter between Odysseus and Eurymakhos.

57. List the sins the suitors have committed up to this point. How are the serving women party to these sins? Who has been sinned against? How?

Lesson Eight
The Odyssey
Chapters XIX-XXIV

1. **Vocabulary**

   unburnished (burnished)
   draught
   artisan
   vivacity
   maudlin
   callow

2. **Read Chapter XIX, pages 353-372.**

3. Fill out the **Overview Chart** for Chapter XIX.

4. Review: This chapter opens with the line, "Now by Athena's side in the quiet hall..." What actions have just preceded this "*now*"?

5. What happens in lines 1-51?

6. In lines 52-57, what does Odysseus say he intends to do?

7. In lines 64-115, Odysseus has a second encounter with Melantho. Describe this encounter. What do you learn about the character of Melantho? How does Penelope react to Melantho's behavior?

8. In lines 116-374, Odysseus and Penelope talk. Describe their conversation.

9. Describing her attempt to trick the suitors by weaving a shroud for her father-in-law, Penelope tells how she was betrayed.

> So every day I wove on the great loom,
> but every night by torchlight I unwove it;
> and so for three years I deceived the Ahkaians.
> But when the seasons brought a fourth year on,
> as long months waned, and the long days were
> spent, through impudent folly in the slinking maids
> they caught me — clamored up to me at night;
> I had no choice but to finish it. (lines 175-182)

What does this tell Odysseus about both his wife and her servant girls?

10. When Penelope orders her servants to prepare a bath for Odysseus, what does he insist on? Why do you think he demands this?

11. Who is Eurykleia? What is she like?

12. Who is Eurynome?

13. What is the significance of the scar on Odysseus' thigh? How did he get it, and why is it significant to the story now?

14. After his bath, Penelope wants to talk some more (lines 591-695). Describe Penelope's dream. How does Odysseus interpret it?

15. What contest does Penelope propose to the disguised Odysseus? How does he respond?

16. **Vocabulary**
    brach
    megaron
    impediment
    tripe

17. **Read Chapter XX, pages 375-387.**

18. Fill out the **Overview Chart** for Chapter XX.

19. In lines 1-22, Odysseus lies down to sleep. What does he witness? How does he react to it?

20. In lines 23-60, who appears to Odysseus? Describe their conversation.

21. In lines 61-101, tell about Penelope's prayer. What does she say about Odysseus? The stranger in the hall?

22. Describe Odysseus' prayer to Zeus in lines 102-140. What "tokens" or assurances does he receive that Zeus has heard and will grant his prayer?

23. In lines 141-180, Telemachus enters the hall (and we also witness the morning chore routine). What do you learn about him? His attitudes? His character?

24. Three servants appear on the scene. Describe each of them, particularly their behavior toward Odysseus—

The swineherd, Eumaios:

The goatherd, Melanthios:

The cowherd, Philoitios:

25. In lines 266-267, what omen do we see?

26. As we, the readers, see this omen, what are the suitors still plotting? Who talks them out of it?

27. How does Ktesippos further insult Odysseus?

28. Tell the significance of the following lines. Also, tell who spoke them.

> O lost men, what terror is this you suffer?
> Night shrouds you to the knees, your heads, your faces
> dry retch of death runs round like fire in sticks;
> Your cheeks are streaming; these fair walls and pedestals
> are dripping crimson blood. And thick with shades
> is the entry way, the courtyard thick with shades
> passing athirst toward Erebos, into the dark,
> the sun is quenched in heaven, foul mist hems us in...

29. How do the suitors respond to this passage? What does the speaker do?

30. From line 428 to the end of this chapter, the poet creates an interesting visual effect. He changes the reader's view of the action by moving the reader's attention from character to character. Reread this section and describe the effect these changes create.

31. **Vocabulary**
    torsion
    dithering

32. **Read Chapter XXI, pages 391-405.**

33. Fill out the **Overview Chart** for Chapter XXI.

34. In lines 1-90, Penelope and her servants retrieve Odysseus' bow and bring it to the hall. Describe each person's response to the bow as they touch it for the first time.

35. And how does Antinoos respond? What does that reveal about his character?

36. While the suitors are struggling with the bow, Odysseus goes outside and talks with the swineherd and the cowherd. What do they talk about?

37. According to Eurymakhos, what ultimate insult does the suitors' inability to string Odysseus' bow represent?

38. Tell about the interchange between Penelope and the suitors in lines 350 - 386. What do we learn about them from these conversations?

39. Describe the scene as Odysseus takes the bow.

40. Tell the speaker and the significance of the following lines:

    Telemakhos, the stranger
    you welcomed in your hall has not disgraced you.
    I did not miss, neither did I take all day
    stringing the bow. My hand and eye are sound,
    not so contemptible as the young men say.
    The hour has come to cook their lordship's mutton ---

41. Tell how the scene closes. What effect does this closing have on the reader?

42. **Vocabulary**
   aegis
   eyries

43. **Read Chapter XXII, pages409-42**
   (but not on a full stomach.)

44. Fill out the **Overview Chart** for Chapter XXII.

45. Who dies first?

46. As soon as Eurymakhos realizes that the stranger is indeed
   Odysseus and that Antinoos died because Odysseus meant to
   kill him and to exact revenge on all the suitors, what does
   Eurymakhos say? What does this tell us about his
   character?

47. What happens to the goatherd, Melanthios?

48. Why does Odysseus refuse to show mercy to Leodes?
   Compare Leodes with another seer met in Chapter XX.

49. Whose lives are spared?

50. Find the lines that tell why the suitors were all killed.
    Write them down below.

51. How many of the women servants were in league with the
    suitors? What is their fate?

52. How does this chapter end? What is the emotional tone?

53. **Vocabulary - Define this word.**
    bordel

54. **Read Chapter XXIII, pages 429-441.**

55. Fill out the **Overview Chart** for Chapter XXIII.

56. Describe Eurykleia's announcement to Penelope. How does Penelope respond? What does that tell us about her?

57. Describe their first meeting (lines 94-109). What is each feeling? What does each do?

58. When Telemakhos scolds his mother, how does she defend herself? How does Odysseus defend her? What does that tell you about each of them?

59. How does Odysseus keep the news of the slaughter from spreading into the town? Why does he want to keep the news from spreading?

60. How does Penelope test Odysseus? Does he pass it?

61. How does Penelope explain her initial coldness?

62. Describe their reunion.

63. What errand does Odysseus leave for at the end of Chapter XXIII?

64. **Read Chapter XXIV, pages 445-462.**

65. Fill out the **Overview Chart** for Chapter XXIV.

66. How does Agamemnon respond to the suitors' news about Odysseus' return?

67. Describe Odysseus' reunion with his father.

68. How does the town react to the news of the slaughter of their sons? How is this conflict resolved?

FINAL ASSIGNMENT FOR *THE ODYSSEY*

Write an essay on one of the following topics.

In what ways is Odysseus an epic hero?

Describe his relationship with the gods and goddesses of Ancient Greece. Compare Odysseus' relationship with the Greek gods with Gilgamesh's relationship with his gods.

Compare Odysseus with Gilgamesh. How are they alike? How are they different? Which hero do you admire more? Identify with more? Which story did you enjoy more?

Choose a person from Israel's history that seems to you to be an example of an epic hero. (Be sure and explain how that person functions as an epic hero.) Then compare that person to either Gilgamesh or Odysseus.

Lesson Nine
Oedipus Rex

Background to Greek Theater

Ancient Greek theater was very different from today's theater.

In Athens plays were generally performed as a part of an annual religious festival held in honor of Dionysos. The plays were held in a semicircular outdoor amphitheater that held over 10,000 people. While there obviously was no sound system, the design of the theater provided excellent acoustics. In tragedies, men played both male and female roles, wearing large masks that represented the character being portrayed. (The shape of the mouthpiece on these masks also helped to project the actors' voices.)

The tragedies were performed over a three-day period. Each playwright would present three tragedies. The tragedies were based on mythological stories. Initially, the chorus was made up of a group of costumed and masked people who would recite poetry based on Greek mythology. Eventually, actors were added. But only two or three actors with speaking parts were allowed on stage at the same time. All violent action happened off stage, and then was described by someone who had witnessed or heard about it. The chorus sometimes functioned as a narrator who filled the audience in on what was happening or was about to happen. Sometimes the chorus commented on the action of the play. Occasionally, the chorus would take part directly in the action.

The Tragic Hero
The hero of a tragedy was a man or woman who was a respected, noble person who possessed some character flaw that would eventually bring about his or her downfall. Often the flaw was pride, sometimes it was anger, and sometimes it was rash behavior. As you read, try to identify both the tragic hero and the tragic flaw.

Lesson Nine
Oedipus Rex
Background and Prologue

Background Information

As you read *Oedipus Rex*, you will see the people of Thebes referred to as the "Children of Cadmus." Read "Cadmus and the Dragon's Teeth" (taken from *Famous Men of Greece)* to find out why—

Cadmus and the Dragon's Teeth

King Agenor and his queen lived in the land Asia, in a country named Phoenicia. They had four children – three sons and a beautiful daughter named Europa.

One morning, as the young people were playing in a meadow near the seashore, a snow-white bull came toward them. Europa and her brothers thought it would be a fine frolic to take a ride on the back of the bull. The brothers agreed that Europa should have the first ride. In a moment she was on the bull's back, and the bull was capering over the meadow. Then suddenly, he ran down to the shore and plunged into the sea. For a little while he could be seen swimming through the water with Europa clinging to his horns. Then both disappeared, and Europa never saw her brothers or her father or mother again. Still, her fate was not a sad one. At the end of a long ride on the back of the bull, she reached that part of the world which to this day is called Europe in her honor. There she married a king and lived happily until her death.

In her old home, however, there was great distress. Agenor sent his sons to look for her and told them not to return until they had found their sister. Their mother went with them. After a long time, the two elder sons gave up the search and settled in a strange land. The mother and the youngest son, Cadmus, wandered on until her death. With her last breath she made him promise to go to Mount Parnassus and ask the oracle where he might find Europa. As soon as she was dead, Cadmus made haste to Parnassus. When he arrived at the mountain, he found the cleft in the rocks from which the oracle had once come to Deucalion. Cadmus stood before the stream of gas that poured from it and asked for advice.

From the cleft came a deep roaring sound. Then he heard the puzzling words, "Follow the cow; and build a city where she lies down."

Cadmus saw a cow nibbling tufts of grass by the roadside, not far from where he was standing. He decided to follow her and, with some of his companions, set out on his journey.

For a long time it seemed as though the cow would not lie down at all. Finally, she began to double her knees under her; as cows do, and in a second more she was at rest on the ground. Cadmus and his men decided to camp on the spot for the night. They looked about for some water and found a spring bubbling out from under a rock.

Now this was really an enchanted spring. It was guarded by a dragon that had the claws of a lion, the wings of an eagle, and the jaws of a serpent. When Cadmus and his men came near, the dragon sprang from behind the rock and killed all but Cadmus.

When the dragon, with wide-open jaws, flew at Cadmus, he thrust his sword down the fiery throat and into the creature's heart. The monster fell dead. Through the air rang the words, "Sow the teeth of the dragon, O Cadmus!"

Though he saw that it would be hard work to break the great teeth out of the dragon's jaws, Cadmus at once set about the task. When it was finished, he dug the soil with the point of his sword as best he could and planted half of the monster's teeth.

Never had grown such a wonderful crop. For every tooth that was planted, a warrior, armed and eager to fight, sprang up. Cadmus gazed in amazement, until a voice in the air commanded, "Throw a stone among the warriors."

Cadmus obeyed and immediately every warrior drew his sword and attacked one of his companions. The woods rang with the din of the battle. One by one the warriors fell, until only five were left. Cadmus now shouted loudly to them, "Be at peace!" When they stopped fighting, he added, "Building is better than killing!"

The warriors agreed, and all set to work to build a city. They called the city Thebes.

So why does the playwright describe the people of Thebes as the "children of Kadmos?"

Lesson Nine – *Oedipus Rex*, Background & Prologue

When the theater-goers attended *Oedipus Rex,* they were already familiar with the story. Below you will find a summary of the things they already knew about Oedipus. Read the summary before you begin reading the play.

The Story of Oedipus

When Laius, the king of Thebes, learned that he and his wife, Jocasta, soon would have a child, he went to the oracle to ask about the child's future. The prophecy he received was far from comforting. It said that the child would one day kill his father and marry his mother. When the child was born, his parents had his legs pinned together at (or through) the ankles. Then he was taken to a secluded hillside and left to die. As often happens in such legends, the man entrusted with this mission found himself unable to leave the child to a slow and certain death. Taking pity on the doomed child, Jocasta's trusted shepherd gave the child to another shepherd who gave the child to the childless king and queen of Corinth. The couple received the child enthusiastically, named him Oedipus (which means, *swollen foot*), and raised him as their own dear son.

Oedipus grew happily, never suspecting that the man and woman who raised him were not his real parents. One day, however, the young man, Oedipus, was insulted by a man who rudely questioned his relationship to Corinth's royal family. Furious, Oedipus charged off to consult the oracle. He was told that he would one day kill his father and marry his own mother. Horrified at the thought, and wanting to make certain that the prophecy could never come to pass, Oedipus left Corinth immediately.

Oedipus reasoned that the best way to avoid fulfilling the prophecy would be to remove himself from Corinth forever. Unfortunately, it was not to be that easy. As Oedipus reached a narrow crossroad, he met a crotchety old man who roughly ordered him to get off the road. In the fight that followed, Oedipus killed that man and several of his attendants. He then continued his journey, thinking nothing more about the incident.

As he approached the city of Thebes, he met another obstacle—the Sphinx that had tormented the city for years. This Sphinx had blocked the road, refusing to let any traveler pass until that person answered his riddle correctly. Here is the riddle:

> What walks on four legs in the morning,
> Two legs at noon,
> And three legs at evening?

Those who failed to answer correctly (and everyone who tried failed) were destroyed. Oedipus, however, answered correctly. Furious that someone had actually guessed his riddle, the Sphinx threw himself off a cliff (Bullies are often known for their bad tempers and lack of self-control.) The city was free!!

Grateful to Oedipus for delivering them, they welcomed him into the city and insisted that he marry their newly widowed queen, Jocasta (spelled Iocasta, in your translation). A-HA! You say? The two marry, bear four children together (Eteocles, Polynices, Ismene and Antigone), and are quite happy UNTIL a mysterious plague strikes the city.

As the play, *Oedipus Rex* begins, the people are praying for relief from this plague.

How the Play is Organized

Look at page 1 of your text. (You have to count back from page 4, which IS numbered in order to realize that this is, indeed, page 1.) It is the table of contents for the play. Each section of the play has a certain function.

The Prologue presents the opening scene of the play. In Greek tragedy the prologue will usually give you any background information that the playwright feels you need in order to follow the action of the play. The prologue prepares you for the action that is to follow.

In **The Parados**, the chorus makes its first entrance. The chorus' first speech will be some expression of the main themes present within the play. Read this section carefully.

In your translation, the next section is called a **scene**, sometimes, though, it is called an **episode**. In this section the plot is developed using action and dialogue between the actors. Sometimes the chorus (the choragos) has a minor role. Each **scene** or **episode** is followed by a **choral ode**. A choral ode is recited by the chorus. As you read the play you are to try and discover the function of the choral ode. Bonus points to the ones who do!

The Exodos is the final scene from the play. At the end all the players make a final *exit (or exodus)*.

Who appears in the play

Now look at page 3 of your text of *Oedipus Rex*. Read the list of "Persons Represented." These are the characters who will make an appearance in the play. (People who only make very brief appearances are not listed.)

Before you begin reading, get out your *Scene Summary Sheet* (found on page   ) and list the people on stage during the first scene.

The Prologue

1. Turn to page   and read the description of the scene before you. Picture it in your mind. Draw a sketch of it in the space below.

2. Be able to identify or define each of the following. If you run across other unfamiliar words, be sure to look them up and record the definitions. If you don't know what the words mean, the play will not make much sense to you (and it won't be Sophocles' fault!)

People and Places
        Kadmos (Cadmos)
        Apollo
        Sphinx
        Delphi

Vocabulary

        prologue
        strewn
        garlands
        preys
        crave
        chaplets
        death surge
        pyre
        battens
        flinty
        citadels
        enquiry
        pilgrimage
        resolve
        highwaymen
        faction
        compunction

3.   **Read *The Prologue*, pages 3-10.**

4.   Describe the scene as the play opens.

5.   Who is present?

6.   What problem is presented?

7. Who do the people come to for help? Why do they come to this person?

8. How does this person respond to the people's request?

9. What does the way he responds tell you about the kind of person he is?

10. How would you describe him?

11. Tell about Creon's trip to Delphi. Who sent him and why was he sent?

12. What does Creon learn at Delphi?

13. How does Oedipus respond to Creon's news?

Lesson Ten
Oedipus Rex
Parados and Scene I

1. Be able to define or identify the following:

People and Places
Phoibos
Artemis
Delphic voice of Zeus
Kithairon

Vocabulary
profound
unjoins
besieger
ravage
edict
propose
lurking
wretchedness
culprit
begetting
ordained
expedient
clairvoyant
pestilence
exile
divination
insolence
infamy
decrepit
mummery
exorcist

2. **Read the Parodos, pages 10-12.**

      a. On your *"Oedipus* **Overview Chart**," pages 140-142, list those who speak in this section. Also record the speaker's main concern.

      b. Why is this section here? What function does the Parodos serve within the play?

3. **Read Scene I, pages 12-24.**

4. List the characters appearing in this scene. Also describe the main action that occurs in this scene on your *"Oedipus Overview Chart."*

5. How much of the chorus' prayer does Oedipus overhear?

6. How does Oedipus respond?

7. What does he proclaim?

8.   Who is Tireseus?

9.   How is Tireseus described? Who called him to Thebes, and why was he called?

10. How does Oedipus respond to Tireseus? What does Oedipus' reaction tell you about his character?

11. How does Tireseus respond to Oedipus? What does Tireseus's reaction tell you about his character?

12. In a distinctive way, mark every occurrence of the word, *blind* or *blindness,* in this section. Continue to do this throughout the entire play.

13. In a distinctive way, mark every occurrence of the word, *truth,* in this section. Continue to do this throughout the play.

> # KNOW THIS ABOUT DRAMATIC IRONY:
>
> **DRAMATIC IRONY** occurs when the character in a play makes a statement that he or she innocently believes to be truth, while the audience is very much aware that the character is either ignorant or deceived.
>
> **DRAMATIC IRONY** also occurs when a character unknowingly (without understanding how true a statement really is) says something that the audience knows is true about that character.

14. How many examples of **DRAMATIC IRONY** can you find in this scene? Describe them, explaining how they are dramatically ironic.

15. THINK! ANALYZE! BE REWARDED ROYALLY!
     How does the playwright build the tension as the scene progresses?

OEDIPUS OVERVIEW CHART

Section	MAIN CHARACTERS	MAIN EVENTS OR CONCERN	COMMENTS
PARADOS			
SCENE I			
ODE I			
SCENE II			

Section	MAIN CHARACTERS	MAIN EVENTS OR CONCERN	COMMENTS
ODE II			
SCENE III			
ODE III			
SCENE IV			

Section	MAIN CHARACTERS	MAIN EVENTS OR CONCERN	COMMENTS
ODE IV			
EXODOS			
QUESTIONS & NOTES			

Lesson Eleven
Oedipus Rex
Ode I and Scene II

1. Be able to define/identify the following:

   People/Places
   Furies
   Parnassos
   Helios

   Vocabulary
   regicide
   avail
   carrion
   diviner
   brazen
   onset
   anarchy
   resolved
   malice
   soothsayer
   maundering
   shrine
   malediction
   tally
   marauder
   ode

2. **Read Ode I, pages 24-25.**
   On your "**Oedipus Overview Chart**," record the speaker of the ode.
   Also record the main concerns expressed in the ode.

3. **Read Scene II, pages 25-43.**
   On your "**Oedipus Overview Chart**," record the characters that
   appear in this scene. Record the main things that happen in this
   section.

4. What do you learn about Creon in this scene? What are his concerns?

5.   What is he upset about and why is he upset about it?

6.   Describe his conversation with Oedipus.

7.   Does either man owe an apology? Who and to whom?

8. Read Creon's speech very carefully, beginning at the last two lines of page 29, and continuing through the bottom of page 30. It contains important information for this play, and we will refer back to it when we read *Antigone*.

9. What do we learn about Creon through this speech?

10.   What could/should Oedipus learn or take to heart from this speech?

11. How does he respond to it? What does his response tell you about his character?

12. What does Creon mean when he says (page 34),

    "Natures like yours chiefly torment themselves."

13. Do you think he is correct? Explain your answer.

14. What role does the Choragos play throughout this scene? What advice does he give Oedipus?

15. Describe Jocasta's reaction to all that she hears and observes. What do her responses tell us about her?

Lesson Twelve
Oedipus Rex
Ode II, Scene III, & Ode III

1. **Vocabulary (DO NOT SKIP!!!)**

    lowly
    realm
    begot
    plummet
    comely
    ordinance
    disdain
    levity
    due earnings
    impious
    obscurities
    suppliant
    overwrought
    helmsman
    isthmus
    sepulcher

2. **Read Ode II, pages 44-45.**
   - On your "**Oedipus Overview Chart**," record the main characters in the ode.
   - Record the main concerns expressed there.
   - Continue to mark any references to blindness/sight or truth in a distinctive way.

3. **Read Scene III, pages 45-57.**
   - On your "**Oedipus Overview Chart**", record the main characters that appear in the scene.
   - Record the main actions/events occurring in the scene.
   - Continue to mark references to blindness and to truth in distinctive ways.

4. To whom does Iocasta/Jocasta speak as she enters at the beginning of Scene III? What is she doing? What is her purpose?

5. What message does the Messenger bear? Is it good news? Defend your answer.

6. How does Iocasta/Jocasta respond to the news? How does Oedipus respond?

7. What do they initially think the news means for them?

8. What do Iocasta/Jocasta's and Oedipus' responses to the news reveal about their characters?

9. What does Oedipus still fear, however? Why?

10. How does Iocasta/Jocasta respond to this fear?

11. In an attempt to relieve Oedipus' fear, the messenger reveals what news?

12. What effect does this news have on Oedipus and Iocasta/Jocasta?

13. How does this news help move the action of the play forward?

14. How does Iocasta/Jocasta respond to this information? Why does she respond this way?

15. Why does Oedipus *think* Iocasta/Jocasta is responding in this way?

16. What is this significance of the Choragos' response to Iocasta/Jocasta's exit on page 56?

17. What is the mood of the play at the end of the scene? How does the writer accomplish this?

18. **Read Ode III, pages 56-57.**

19. What question does the chorus ask in this passage? Record your answer on your "**Oedipus Overview Chart.**"

Lesson Thirteen
Oedipus Rex
Scene IV, Ode IV, & Exodos

1. **Vocabulary**

   pasturage
   recollection
   wretched
   void
   renown
   venerate
   daemon
   shroud
   rank/ rankness
   execrable
   engendered
   reproach
   affront
   parricide
   purge
   bane
   beggary

2. **Read Scene IV, pages 57-63.**
   - On your "**Oedipus Overview Chart**", record the main characters appearing in the scene.
   - Also record the main actions/events that occur.
   - Continue to mark all references to *blindness* and *truth* in the text of the play.

3. Who does Oedipus speak to at the opening of the scene?

4. What does Oedipus want to find out from the shepherd?

5.   Why is the shepherd reluctant to answer his question?

6.   How much of the situation does the Messenger understand?

7.   What effect does the Messenger's level of understanding have on the mood of the scene? On the way we feel toward the Messenger?

Discuss its *dramatic* effect.

8.   Who does the shepherd say gave him the child? What is your response to that news? Would you respond differently if Laius had given the child to the shepherd? Why?

9.   How does Oedipus respond specifically to *this* information?

10. How does Oedipus respond to the news that the prophecies were, in fact, true?

11. How does he describe himself at the end of the scene?

12. **Read Ode IV, page 63-65.**
    - On your "Oedipus Overview Chart", record the speaker and the main concerns expressed in this ode.
    - Who is talked about?
    - What is said?

13. **Read Exodos, pages 65-78.**
    - On your "Oedipus Overview Chart", record the main characters appearing in this scene.
    - Also, record the main actions/events occurring here.
    - Continue to mark all references to *blindness* and *truth*.

14. Who speaks at the beginning of the scene?

15. What new information does that speaker bring?

16. How is this announcement made? What dramatic effect is created by making this announcement so brief?

17. Where does all the violent action take place?

18. What effect does that have dramatically?

19. What advantage does this have over our witnessing these actions first hand? How does it leave us feeling as Oedipus makes his entrance?

20. What does the Choragos mean by the following statement?

> "This is not strange,
>   You suffer it all twice over, remorse in pain
>   Pain in remorse."

21. Whom does Oedipus hold responsible for his blindness and his fate?

22.   How accurate is Oedipus?

23.   The final words of the Choragos are:

> *This is the king who solved the famous riddle*
> *And towered up, most powerful of men.*
> *No mortal eyes but looked on him with envy,*
> *Yet in the end ruin swept over him.*
>
> *Let every man in mankind's frailty*
> *Consider his last day: and let none*
> *Presume on his good fortune until he find*
> *Life, at his death, a memory without pain.*

What do these words mean?

ESSAY QUESTION

Is Oedipus merely a tragic victim of fate or does he bear some responsibility for what has happened to him? Does he have a tragic character flaw that contributes to his end? If so, what is that flaw and *how much* does it contribute to his end?

As you work toward an answer to these questions, use the chart on the next page. List the reasons why you could say Oedipus is at fault. Next, list the reasons why you could call him an innocent victim of Fate. Cite specific examples from the play that support each reason.

Now answer this question in an essay.

OEDIPUS AT FAULT	OEDIPUS THE VICTIM

INQUIRING MINDS WANT TO KNOW THE PURPOSE OF THE CHORAL ODES

In the **choral ode**, the Chorus comments on the contents of the scene they've just witnessed, and so provides commentary. Sometimes the chorus seems to speak for the gods, or speak a truth that the characters in the play seem to have missed. Sometimes, they will speak for those watching—either those within the play who are looking on or those in the audience who are watching. See, it wasn't all that hard...

Lesson Fourteen
Antigone by Sophocles
Background from *Oedipus at Colonus*, Prologue, Parados, Scene I, & Ode I

1. Look at the list of "Persons Represented" found at the top of page 185. Which of them were also represented in *Oedipus Rex?* (List them below.)

2. What do you know about the character or personality of each?

3. Read Creon's description of himself in *Oedipus*, p. 30. Copy it down below beginning on page 29 with the words, *"Would any sane. . ."* and ending with *"and never would deal with any man who likes it."*

4. Does Creon want to be king? What does he like about being king?

   What is he happy to do without?

5. What is anarchy? What does Creon's comment about anarchy tell you
   about the kind of person he is? What would you expect him to be like?

6. In the second of the three Oedipus plays, Creon appears again. If you have
   time to read the entire play, you would find helpful bits of information
   about the relationships between the major characters there. In case you
   do not, read the following summary of the play.

Oedipus at Colonus

   Twenty years after Oedipus has left Thebes in disgrace, we find him
about a mile northwest of the city of Athens in the grove of the Furies at
Colonus. He is accompanied by his daughter Antigone and we learn that
she has been her father's faithful companion, his "eyes," so to speak, for
quite a while. As the play opens he rests on a rock. A stranger warns him
that he is on holy ground and should move. He agrees to let the people of
Colonus know the old man is there and summon Theseus, king of Athens.
   In the Choral Dialogue, the Chorus enters looking for the "impious,
blasphemous, shameless" stranger. When Oedipus shows himself to them,

they demand that he tell them his name and story. After they know who he is they forget earlier promises of hospitality and demand that he leave before his curse rubs off on them. On pages 95-96, Oedipus attempts to defend himself, telling his side of the story.

Impressed, the chorus agrees to withhold judgment, passing that job onto "higher authorities." At this point Ismene, Oedipus' other daughter, arrives with news that Thebes now wants Oedipus to return—sort of.

In his greeting he reveals something of his relationship with his two sons.

> They behave as if they were Egyptians,
> Bred the Egyptian way! Down there, the men
> Sit indoors, all day long, weaving!
> The women go out and tend to business.
> Just so your brothers, who should have done this work
> Sit by the fire like home-loving girls,
> And you two, in their place, must bear my hardships.
>   (pp. 99-100)

Ismene comes to tell Oedipus of his sons' troubles. Eteocles, the younger brother, has stripped Polyneices, the older brother, of his position and banished him. He has fled to Argos and gathered an army, preparing an attack on Thebes. She also brings word of a new oracle concerning Oedipus.

It seems that the oracle has predicted that if Oedipus were buried near Thebes, his burial site would also be the site of a military victory. If he were not buried there, Thebes would suffer military defeat. Oedipus arranges with Theseus to be buried honorably near Athens, rejecting the call "home." Told that he must offer sacrifices to the Furies (or Eumenides) for his trespass on a holy spot, Ismene goes into the woods to make the required libations.

In Scene III, Theseus arrives and promises Oedipus that he may live safely under his protection and be honorably buried there when he dies. In Scene IV, Creon arrives and the fur flies. Read his greeting to Oedipus, pages 121-122. How does Oedipus respond to him? Finish reading this scene.

7. How would you describe Creon's concern for Oedipus? Are Oedipus' suspicions and hostility justified? Support your answer.

8. When it is clear that Oedipus will not return willingly to Thebes, what does Creon do?

9. Describe Oedipus' curse (p. 129).

10.   On pages 131-133, Theseus reprimands Creon for "dragging helpless people from their sanctuary."   How does Creon defend himself? Do you buy his defense? Why or why not?

11. Read Oedipus' response to Creon's comments. How does he defend himself and his actions? Are you convinced that his descriptions are accurate? Are the Athenians convinced?

    • How does he describe/defend his murder of his father: (Compare this with the story he originally told in *Oedipus Rex*, p. 41.)

    • How does he describe/defend his marriage to Jocasta:

12. Theseus orders Creon to accompany him and restore Antigone and Ismene to him. Once they are all reunited, word comes that Oedipus has still another visitor, his son, Polyneices. Oedipus gives him an icy reception. Polyneices explains that he has been betrayed and exiled by his younger brother. He has taken refuge and gathered an army, but knows from the oracle that those who secure Oedipus' favor will prevail. Thus, he comes to Oedipus to seek his favor, and thus succeed against his brother.

    Oedipus is displeased (understatement!) that neither of the sons have sought him out before now – leaving all the hardship to their two sisters. Oedipus disowns and curses Polyneices

>   Go with the malediction
>   I here pronounce for you: that you shall never
>   Master your native land by force of arms,
>   Nor see your home again in Argos,
>   The land below the hills; but you shall die
>   By your own brother's hand, and you shall kill
>   The brother who banished you. For this I pray.

The Greenleaf Guide to Ancient Literature

13. Read the rest of this scene and answer the following questions.

    - Describe Antigone's relationship with Polyneices.

    - What request does Polyneices make of his sisters?

14. In **Scene VII**, Oedipus summons Theseus to tell him that he will die soon. Promising to tell Theseus what the future holds for Athens, Oedipus charges him never to reveal the place of his death and burial. Telling his daughters good-bye, he makes a hasty exit.

    In the **Choral Dialogue** that follows **Scene VIII**, the Chorus tells the girls about his death and attempts to comfort them. At the end of the scene, Theseus arrives and refuses the girls' request to see their father's resting site. Antigone agrees to be satisfied to obey her father's dying request for secrecy, asking Theseus to

    > Send us back, then, to ancient Thebes,
    > And we may stop the bloody war
    > from coming between our brothers!

    Turn to the first page of *Antigone*. Read the description of the scene. As *Antigone* begins, what has just happened?

    How successful, then, have Antigone and Ismene been in stopping the civil war?

15. **Read the *Prologue, Parados, Scene I,* and *Ode I.***
    (An *"Antigone* Overview Chart" can be found on pages 180-182. If you found that completing the chart helped you as you read the previous play, use it again. If you and your teacher agree that you don't need it, just pretend it is not there.)

    As you read, **mark any references to *LAW*** in some distinctive way.

16. **Vocabulary**

> carrion
> eddy
> marshaled
> helms
> sate/sated
> swaggers
> arc
> auspicious
> doddering
> anarchist
> anarchy
> sultry

> Dirce's stream- a spring of water located near the city of Thebes.

17. What request does Antigone make of Ismene?

18. How does she respond? What reasons does she give for her response?

19. How would you describe the two sisters? How are they alike? How are they different?

20.   Describe Creon's decree.

21.   Why is Antigone so determined to defy Creon?

22.   What happens during any *parados*?

      In this *Parados* what is discussed?

23.   Describe the battle in your own words. (Be detailed.)

24.   What characters are found in Scene I?

25. What announcement does Creon make in Scene I?

26. How does the Choragos react?

27. How would you describe the Sentry? What report does he bring?

28. Why does the Choragos say, " I have been wondering, King: can it be that the gods have done this?"

29. Why does Creon respond so strongly to that possibility, do you think?

30. Describe Antigone and Creon. How are they alike? How are they different? What kind of person is each? Write at least one well-written, well-supported paragraph describing each character.

Lesson Fifteen
Antigone by Sophocles
Scene II & Ode II

1. List the characters that appear in Scene II.

2. **Read Scene II and Ode II, pages 205-216, for this lesson.**

3. **Vocabulary**

    insolence
    brazen
    crest (cresting)
    lull

4. Think dramatically here. As the sentry is making his long
    speech about how clever he has been in catching Antigone *in
    the very act* of burying her brother, what function is he
    serving dramatically? OR, what *dramatic effect* is he
    having?

5. At the end of *Oedipus Rex,* what request did Oedipus make of
    Creon on behalf of Antigone and Ismene?

6. Describe Creon's attitude and his apparent relationship with
    Antigone and Ismene. What do we learn about his character
    through this?

7. Describe Antigone—her reaction to being caught, to Creon, her defense of herself. What do we learn about her character through these things?

8. Describe Antigone's relationship with Ismene. Look back to the observations you made about the two girls as you observed them in the Prologue. What might you add after reading this scene? Would you change any of your observations or conclusions based on your reading in this scene? Do the things you see in this scene confirm anything you thought you saw in the Prologue? Be specific about why you would or would not make changes.

9. With what is Creon most concerned?

10. With what is Antigone most concerned?

11. Is there any middle ground (a place to compromise) between their two positions?

12. What family ties does Creon reject in Scene II?

13. What does he value above those things you listed in #12?

14. Time to think beyond the obvious here. As you have read so far, you probably have found yourself siding with either Creon or Antigone. I want you to look carefully and critically at the actions, intentions, and motivations of each character. Is Creon acting nobly or being a jerk? Is Antigone acting nobly or selfishly?

Wherever your sympathies lie, I want you to see how you might build a case for both interpretations using specific examples (actions, events, lines) from the text of the play.

Creon is noble.

Creon is a jerk.

Antigone is noble.

Antigone is a selfish spoiled brat.

15. Now that you have looked at both sides of the question, which position seems to be the strongest? Which character is acting nobly? Which character is *not* acting nobly? (You get to tell what you think they **are** being!)

16. Put yourself in the play. Who do you identify with? Which character would you most likely have been? Explain.

Lesson Sixteen
Antigone by Sophocles
Scene III & Ode III

1. Read Scene III and Ode III.

2. What characters appear in this scene?

3. Read Haimon's conversation with Creon carefully. What can you discern about Creon's philosophy of government? What does he value? What does he see as the ultimate evil for society, and so the greatest crime a person can commit against society?

4. How does Haimon attempt to counter (or argue against) his father's position?

5. How does Creon respond to Haimon's arguments?

6. What does Haimon threaten to do if Antigone dies? Does his father seem to pick up on that threat?

7. What changes does Creon make in his orders at the end of the scene?

8. What do we learn about Creon's character in this scene?

9. **Vocabulary**

deference
malicious
subordinate
brawl
vile
perverse
piety
Aphrodite

10. In Ode III, what does the Chorus say about love?

11. Based on what you have read so far, how would you describe the Chorus? How much does the Chorus seem to understand? How *critically* does the Chorus listen, that is, does the chorus seem to readily accept whatever it hears at face value, or does the Chorus analyze or test what it hears before it accepts it?

Lesson Seventeen
Antigone by Sophocles
Scene IV & Ode IV

1. Sophocles makes references to several mythological stories in this scene. Make sure you know them. (Does this sound like a *strong* suggestion?)

      Acheron

      Niobe

      Tantalus/Tantalos

      Persephone

      Danae

      Dryas and Dionysus

2. Describe the main action of Scene IV.

3. How would you characterize Antigone's comments as she is led away? If you were playing Antigone in a production of the play, how would you deliver these lines? What tone would you use?

171

4. How would you characterize the Chorus' response to Antigone? What is its attitude toward her?

5. At what points do Antigone and the Chorus contradict one another? Write the conflicting lines out below.

6. Describe Creon's behavior through all of this. If you were playing Creon, how would you deliver his lines?

7. **Read Ode IV.**

8. What does the Chorus tell Antigone about as she exits? What point does the Chorus seem to want to make to her?

9. Enough depression for one week. Go eat something chocolate. (The previous instruction is an Official Homework Directive. Do not violate.)

10. But first look up any words used in #9 that you did not understand.

Lesson Eighteen
Antigone by Sophocles
Scene V, Paen & Exodos

1. **Vocabulary**

   augury
   entrails
   welter
   aphorism
   paean
   chorister
   choric
   rapture
   maenads

2. **Read Scene V.**

3. Who appears in Scene V?

4. How does Teiresias know that Creon is standing "on the edge of fate?" How does he know the gods are not pleased?

5. Describe Creon's response to Teiresias. What does this tell us about Creon? Any parallels with previous kings of Thebes?

6. Describe the *arrows* Teiresias leaves for Creon.

7. **Read the Paean**.

8. **Read the Exodus**.

9. **Mark every reference to Fate** in this section.

10. Who appears in the Exodus?

11. Describe the fulfillment of Teiresias' *arrows*.

12. What do the characters say about Fate in the Exodus?

13. Where do all acts of violence take place? Why?

14. Tell the significance of these final four lines to the whole of the play.

> *There is no happiness where there is no wisdom.*
> *No wisdom but in submission to the gods.*
> *Big words are always punished,*
> *And proud men in old age learn to be wise.*

15. Look back at the observations you made about the nobility (or lack of nobility) of Creon and Antigone. Have any of your opinions changed about either person as you have read further in the play? If so, how and why have they changed?

16. Over the years, there has been quite a bit of discussion over who the **tragic hero** of this play really is. Some say Antigone, some say Creon. Review the information about the tragic hero found on page 128 of this study guide.

17. What is a tragic hero?

18. What is a **tragic flaw**?

19. Who is the tragic hero of this play?

20. Identify the hero's tragic flaw.

ESSAY

Write an essay in which you give a detailed answer to questions 17 and 18. Is it Antigone or Creon? Support your answer with specific references to the text of the play.

ANTIGONE OVERVIEW CHART

	MAIN CHARACTERS	MAIN EVENT OR CONCERN	COMMENTS
PROLOGUE			
SCENE I			
ODE I			
SCENE II			

ANTIGONE OVERVIEW CHART

	MAIN CHARACTERS	MAIN EVENT OR CONCERN	COMMENTS
ODE II			
SCENE III			
ODE III			
SCENE IV			

ANTIGONE OVERVIEW CHART

	MAIN CHARACTERS	MAIN EVENT OR CONCERN	COMMENTS
ODE IV			
SCENE V			
PEAN			
EXODOS			

Lesson Nineteen
Antigone by Anouilh
Pages 3-10

BACKGROUND INFORMATION

Jean Anouilh

Jean Anouilh was born in 1910 in Bordeaux, France. He studied law at the Sorbonne for a little while (one could say *briefly.....joke. You may laugh*). After this, Anouilh held a variety of writing jobs. In 1937, Anouihl's first successful play, *Le Voyageur Sans Bagage* established his reputation as a playwright.

In 1944, Anouilh's *Antigone* was produced in Paris. At that time Paris was occupied by Nazi Germany and ruled by the Vichy government. As you read the play, you'll be looking for reasons why such a play would attract a large audience.

Anouilh was influenced by Satre's existentialism. He wrote in a wide variety of styles – realistic, fantasy, historical, and absurdist plays. His popularity increased through the forties and fifties, then fell off as drama critics shifted their attention to Ionesco (*The Bald Soprano*) and Samuel Beckett (*Waiting for Godot*). Anouilh died in 1987 in Switzerland. (Trivia: His daughter Catherine Anouilh is an actress, seen in both plays and movies. Just so you'd know!)

Existentialism

Existentialism is a philosophy with roots in the 19th century writings of Nietzsche, Dostoevsky, and Kierkegaard, however, it is primarily a 20th century movement.

In a typical existential world-view

- There are no absolutes, no rational set of facts that govern reality. Everybody's reality is unique to them. What is right for one person in one situation will not be right for any one else. There is no objective or rational base on which to make moral decisions. There is **no** objective right or wrong.
- Life does not have a given meaning or purpose. It has no objective or rational meaning or purpose. What happens to a person is the result of random forces that are impersonal, futile and absurd.
- Each individual makes his own meaning by making choices. The human experience is one of anxiety, guilt, futility, and isolation in an indifferent universe. How a person responds to all that happens around him, will determine his character, his fate. He can act nobly or not.

Existentialism recognizes that all men have a longing for significance, immortality, and meaning, but says that such longings are futile. Because the existential universe is random, indifferent, impersonal, very mortal, those longings will never be satisfied.

Historical Context: A Research ASSIGNMENT

Before you begin the play, you need to do a little historical research. Find out about the time period in which Anouilh wrote the play. What was the Vichy government? How did the Nazi occupation effect life in France?

You might want to watch the video, "Le Chambon." It is in French with English subtitles, and is the story of a small village that conspires to hide Jewish children sent to them from all over France. You can order a copy from Vision Video/Gateway Films.

In order to really understand the way Anouilh is using the story of Antigone, you need to understand the historical context he's writing to. Anouilh's political and philosophic re-interpretation of Antigone will change the ways in which the audience or the readers will respond to each of the different characters.

On to the play...

Unlike the last play you read, this edition of *Antigone* is not divided into scenes. There will be no Choral Odes. (Mourn quietly, please.) Your worksheet, therefore, will refer you to page numbers instead of to acts and scenes.

Chorus Introduces the Characters, pages 3-6.

1. As the play begins, the CHORUS stands alone on stage and introduces you to both the characters you will meet in the play, and to some of the **ideas** expressed in the play. READ THESE THREE PAGES VERY VERY CAREFULLY.

2. **VOCABULARY**

    sallow
    frock
    patron
    premonition
    beset
    cyclorama
    edict

3. Summarize the CHORUS' comments about each of the characters.

    ANTIGONE

    ISMENE

    HAEMON

    CREON

    EURYDICE

NURSE

MESSENGER

ETEOCLES

POLYNICES (Yes, it was spelled differently in the Sophocles, *Antigone*. How clever of you to notice.)

4. How would you describe the CHORUS?

5. How does the CHORUS in this play compare with the Chorus/Choragos we saw in both *Oedipus and* the Sophocles *Antigone*?

ANTIGONE, NURSE, & ISMENE, pages 6-10.

1. **Vocabulary**

   dandle

2. What does Antigone really go out early to do? Why does she need to go secretly?

3. Describe Antigone's conversation with her nurse. How does the nurse misunderstand Antigone? What is the effect of this misunderstanding on the tone of the scene?

Lesson Twenty
Antigone by Anouilh
Pages 10-23

ISMENE & ANTIGONE, pages 10-13

1. By now, we suspect something that Ismene doesn't yet realize. What is it?

2. What have Antigone and Ismene obviously talked about before? What does Antigone want Ismene to do?

3. What is Ismene's response? What reason does she give for her response?

4. How does Antigone react to Ismene? Is she swayed by Ismene's reasoning?

5. Which of the two sisters do you side with? Why?

6. Which of the two sisters is more practical?

7. Which of the two sisters do you admire more?

8. Describe Ismene's character. Does she display any character faults or flaws?

9. Describe Antigone's character. Does she display any character faults or flaws?

10. What do you think is going to be the main conflict of the play?

ISMENE, ANTIGONE, NURSE, HAEMON
(pages 13-20)

1. Throughout the scene, what does Antigone seem to be anticipating? Do the other characters understand her meaning? What effect do these misunderstandings have on the tone of this section of the play?

2. What does Antigone want the nurse to promise her?

3. Describe Antigone's conversation with Haemon. What is she concerned about?

4. How would you describe Haemon? What is he like? How do you feel about him? (Does he seem to be kind, honorable, trustworthy, brutal, deceitful or despicable?)

5. What does Antigone make Haemon promise her?

6. Ismene enters the stage at the end of this section. What is bothering her? What is her final answer to Antigone's request?

7. How does Antigone respond to Ismene?

8. What is the dramatic effect of the scene change following immediately after Antigone's announcement?

CREON, GUARD
(pages 21-23)

1. What news does the guard bring Creon?

2. Describe the guard's behavior. Why does he behave like he does?

3. How does Creon respond to the news? What does his reaction tell us about his character? (This is a question you will need to continue to ask as you read through the play.)

Lesson Twenty-one
Antigone by Anouilh
Pages 23-44

**CHORUS: *"The spring is wound up tight,"* speech
(pages 23-24)**

This speech takes place at a crucial point in the play. Its content is very significant. READ IT CAREFULLY.

1. What does the Chorus tell us about the nature of tragedy? What makes something *tragic*?

2. Why does the Chorus say, "The spring is wound up tight"? How does the image of a tightly wound spring fit his understanding of the nature of tragedy? (You have to think about this one. The answer isn't spelled out *for you* in the text. Stare at the blank space below....or read and re-read the passage until it comes to you....)

3. What does the Chorus say is the difference between tragedy and melodrama?

GUARD, ANTIGONE, CREON
(pages 24-29)

1. What is the dramatic effect of Antigone's entrance at the conclusion of the Chorus' speech?

2. Describe the guards. What are they most concerned with?

3. What is Antigone's reaction to or assessment of them?

4. How do the guards change when Creon walks in? What does that tell you about them?

5. Look back at the Chorus' description of the policemen at the first of the play. Does it appear to be an accurate description of these three men? In what ways yes, in what ways no?

6. Before Creon enters, how do the three guards expect Creon to reward them for capturing Antigone? At the end of the scene, what is Creon thinking about doing to the guards? What does this tell you about Creon?

CREON, ANTIGONE ALONE
(pages 29-43)

1. Describe Creon's attitude toward the Law. Describe his view of a leader's role in society – a leader's responsibility.

2. What is Antigone's attitude toward the Law? How does her view compare with Creon's view?

3. For which character do you feel the most sympathy? Empathy?

4. Which is the tragic hero/heroine – Creon or Antigone? Explain your answer.

5. What does Creon fear?

6. What does Antigone fear?

7. Many references are made to similarities between Oedipus and Antigone. Having read the two other Oedipus plays, do you think Antigone is like her father or not? Explain your answer.

ISMENE, ANTIGONE, CREON, GUARDS
(pages 43-44)

1. Describe Ismene as she enters the stage. What are her concerns at this point? Has she changed any since the last time we saw her? Be specific.

2. How does Antigone react to Ismene's announcement that the two sisters will die together?

3. Why do you think Antigone has this reaction? Do you think her reaction is justified?

4. When Ismene threatens to bury the body for Antigone, the action of the scene intensifies. How does the playwright accomplish this?

5. How does Creon react to Ismene's threat?

Lesson Twenty-two
Antigone by Anouilh
Pages 44-53

CHORUS, CREON, HAEMON
(pages 44-46)

1. From the point where Ismene threatens to bury the body of her brother, tension continues to build as more and more people enter and challenge Creon's decree.
   In the space below –
   - List the names of those who confront Creon.
   - To what does each of these characters appeal?
   - How does Creon respond to them –and how does he justify his behavior?
   - What do Creon's responses tell you about him?

2. Summarize the Chorus' comments to Creon.

3. How does Creon respond?

4. Describe Haemon's conversation with his father. Describe their relationship.

5. Why won't Creon save Antigone?

6. Is it really true that Creon can do nothing to save her? Why do you answer as you do?

7. Describe Creon's understanding of the Law.

ANTIGONE AND THE GUARDS
(pages 46-50)

1. Tell about the conversation Antigone has with the guard on pages 46 through the top of 49. What do you learn about the guard's character?

2. How does Antigone react to news about the details of her death?

3. Why do you think the guard offers to send out for something for Antigone? Does that add anything to or change your understanding of his character? Explain.

4. How does the guard respond to Antigone when the drum begins beating? Why does he respond that way? Again, what does his response reveal about his character?

5. Would you describe the guards as evil?

6. If you put the guards into the historical context of occupied France, does that alter your answer to question #5 in any way? Explain.

MESSENGER, CREON, CHORUS
(pages 51-53)

1. What news does the Messenger bring to the Queen?

2. Notice that all death and mayhem happens offstage in traditional Greek fashion, and is reported to the audience by someone who has witnessed it. What effect does this have on the audience? In what position does that put the audience?

3. How does Creon react to the news of Eurydice's death? Why do you think he responds in this way? How would you expect him to respond? Explain your answer.

4. As the play closes, Creon talks with the page. Why? What does he tell him? What does Creon seem most preoccupied with? Why?

5. What seems to be the relationship between Creon and the page? Do you find anything odd about the conversation?

6. On the last page of the play, the Chorus makes his final speech. Summarize it. What is its tone?

7. As the guards enter the stage again, what do they do? What effect does this have (that is, how does it make you feel? What emotional tone does it create?)

8. How do you think the audience in Paris in 1944 would have interpreted this final scene? How would they have felt toward the guards? Why?

9. What do the Guards symbolize? (Yes, I know. It is not directly answered anywhere in the play. If you did your homework and researched Vichy, France, it shouldn't be all that hard!)

10. Do you want to change your earlier assessment of the guards at this point? Are the guards evil? Explain your answer. Is Creon evil? (To answer either question you are going to have to decide how you would define evil. What makes a person or an action evil?)

Lesson Twenty-three
Antigone by Anouilh
Summary & Review

FINAL DISCUSSION TIME:

Time for deep thought, scrupulous scholarship, and amazing insight!

If you are studying this play with others, use these questions to help you prepare for a final group discussion of *Antigone*. If you are studying it alone, use these questions to help you look at some of the bigger issues raised by this play. These are issues you will find yourself discussing with other people at some point in your life. SO, to prepare yourself for whatever discussion opportunity awaits you, do the following assignment with diligence.

Antigone raises a number of complex questions, so don't be lazy and grab at the first answer that comes to mind. You may use your book and your **Oedipus Overview Charts**, but work through each question thoughtfully.

In addition to preparing you for discussion, these questions will also help you prepare for any final essay assignment your teacher might choose to give you.

Be wise! Work done thoughtfully now will bear much fruit. (Ah Grasshopper! Wise child listen to honorable instructor.)

1. What Law does Creon honor? How do you know?

2. What Law does Antigone honor? How do you know?

3. Which one is correct?

4. Can you think of a time in the Bible when individuals had to choose between obedience to two conflicting laws? When? How did they choose? What did God think of their choices and how do you know?

5. Remember the historical context of Jean Anouilh's *Antigone*. Just for the fun of it, write it down.

6. What does this play have to say to that situation you described in question #5?

7. What does the Bible have to say to that situation?

    You might want to read biographies of Christians like
    Corrie Ten Boom and her family who made some hard and
    costly choices during that time. What did Corrie Ten Boom
    have to say to that situation?)

8. In that historical context, what do each of the following
    symbolize or represent?

    Antigone

    Creon

    the guards

    Ismene

Eurydice, Haemon, the Nurse

the page

9. List Antigone's and Creon's strengths and weaknesses below.

Antigone
Strengths

Weaknesses

Creon
Strengths

Weaknesses

10. What makes something *tragic* according to the Ancient Greeks?

11. What was the tragedy of Sophocles' *Antigone*?

12. What makes something *tragic* according to Anouilh?

13. What was the tragedy of Anouilh's *Antigone?*

14. How has the concept of tragedy changed between the two plays?

15. Who was the tragic hero/heroine in Sophocles' *Antigone?*

16. Who was the tragic hero/heroine in Anouilh's *Antigone*? (Remember to take this play's historical context into account as you think this question through. Think about who each character represents. How is each of those characters heroic or **not** heroic?)

17. In order to really answer questions 9-12 intelligently, you need to understand something about the existential worldview. Review the introductory material on pages 183-184, and do whatever outside research you need to do in order to be able to summarize the basic tenets of existentialism.

18. How has the worldview seemed to have changed between the Ancient Greeks and the Existentialists?

19. How have these changes affected the concept of *heroism*? How is the Ancient Greek tragic hero expected to behave?

How is the existential hero expected to behave

20. Is there anything else that strikes you about the play?

21. Are there any questions you would like to discuss further with your teacher or your class?

Lesson Twenty-Four
FINAL FINAL DISCUSSION

At the beginning of this study guide (page 3-4) is a list of issues that you have been encouraged to think through as you have studied this course. Here is the list again:

1. Man's beginnings according to Genesis and Romans 1.
2. The differences between the Biblical account of early man and the evolutionary view.
3. A Biblically based apologetic (or defense) for the study of cultures (ancient ones like Babylon and Greece, in particular) by way of Daniel's example.
4. How God's character differs from the character of the gods of the Babylonians/Sumerians, and Greeks.
5. Heroism. What is a true hero? What makes a person great?
6. Man's relationship to God—(Biblically and in the pagan world).
7. Differences between things like wisdom and cunning.
8. Question of Fate—what determines a man's fate and what can one do to alter that fate? How much responsibility does a person have for the way life turns out?
9. What is the Biblical relationship between the individual and the state and God? What about civil disobedience?

Choose one of these issues and write an essay (or research paper) in which you discuss the question. What would you say to your culture about your topic? (The audience for question number three would be primarily Christian.)

Your culture, your peers, your future instructors even, have their own opinions about all of these issues. At some point, like Daniel before Nebuchadnezzar, you will have an opportunity to "make a defense for the hope that is in you." (1 Peter 3:15) What will you say?

Try to look at this assignment as a way to prepare yourself for those future opportunities, not just another "school thing" someone is making you do. Have fun with it.

Be sure to support your position with detailed and specific references to the literature you have studied this year and to the Scriptures.

You are done. Go celebrate!

Now that you have spent a year studying the literature of the Ancient Greeks, you are officially qualified to answer one last question:

What do you call it when a guy loses his pocket protector, his acne cream, and his internet girlfriend all in one day?

A geek tragedy, of course!